T5-BPY-808

THE FUTURE LIFE ACCORDING
TO ORTHODOX TEACHING

by Constantine Cavarnos

translated by
Hieromonk Auxentios and
Archimandrite Chrysostomos

Foreword by
Archimandrite Chrysostomos

CENTER FOR TRADITIONALIST
ORTHODOX STUDIES

Etna, California 96027

1985

The Greek original of this small book was dedicated by Professor Cavarnos to the venerable memory of his loving parents, Panagiotis and Irene. We repeat here his dedication with a fond note of gratitude to the author for his friendship and to our Bishop, Metropolitan Cyprian, for encouragement in undertaking this publication.

BT
904
.C3813
1985

The Future Life According to Orthodox Teaching originally appeared in Greek under the title, Ἡ Μέλλουσα Ζωὴ κατὰ τὴν Ὀρθόδοξον Διδασκαλίαν, and was published by *Ekdoseis "Orthodoxou Typou"* (Athens, 1984). The present English translation is a slightly different rendering of the Greek original.

Library of Congress Catalog No. 85 - 071586

Copyright 1985 by Center for Traditionalist Orthodox Studies

All rights reserved

ISBN 0-911165-06-1

TABLE OF CONTENTS

A SELECTION OF BOOKS

by Constantine Cavarnos

Anchored in God: Life, Art, and Thought on the Holy Mountain of Athos

Plato's View of Man

A Dialogue Between Bergson, Aristotle, and Philologos

Modern Greek Philosophers on the Human Soul

Byzantine Thought and Art

Modern Greek Thought

Plato's Theory of Fine Art

Τὸ Σύμπαν καὶ ὁ Ἄνθρωπος Στὴν Ἀμερικανικὴ Φιλοσοφία

Modern Greek Saints, in eight volumes

Foreword

> ...Ther is Joye in heven and peyne
> in helle; And I accorde wel that hit
> is so; But natheles, yit wot I wel al-
> so, That ther nis noon dwelling in
> this contree, That either hath in he-
> ven or helle y-be, Ne may of hit
> non other weyes witen, But as he
> hath herd seyd, or founde hit writ-
> en.
>
> *Chaucer*

There are few subjects in religious thought so com-
pelling as that of the future life, or life after death. Indeed, there are those who would argue, with a some-
what privative view of the subject, that religion itself
rises out of human desperation at the thought of death
and the compensatory need to seek the afterlife. Just
such a notion well may be the dominant one in a soci-
ety such as ours, which admits theoretically and with a
certain nostalgia to the existence of Eternity, but really
does not predicate life on its existence.

To the Orthodox Christian, the afterlife is an essential part of this life. In our Liturgical life, we attain true
communion with our fellow Christians *only* when that
which is Heavenly is joined with the earthly and the
living join chorus with those gone forth before us. Indeed, the culmination of our Christian life is realized in
the eating and drinking of the flesh and blood of one
Who died, yet still lives, Who brings to death life, and

Who joins the living and dead in the Eternal life of the Resurrection.

In the mystical life of the Church, there is a constant interaction between the Eternal and the time-bound. *Theosis,* in which man reaches his highest state of perfection on earth, being bound in the body yet cleansed of the passions, rests on the constant interplay and interaction of the Eternal world and the world that is subject to death. Participating in the divine, imperfectly communing with the perfect, our Holy Fathers and Saints, who by Grace shine forth even in our day —though in ever fewer numbers—, reveal in their lives a spiritual reality that links every true-believing Orthodox believer to the Eternal. And it is from the sayings, reports, witness, and written words of these holy men and women that we know, too, as much as it is possible to know in darkness what is a pure property of light, something of the nature of the life after death.

In modern times, theology —and, alas, to some extent in the Orthodox Church, too— has become the domain of speculation and creative presumption. We have separated the description of true spiritual experience, which was once real theology, from the modern practice of theology —the modern "doing" of theology that gives forth to   spiritual dilettantism, if not blasphemy, if not, finally, disbelief. So it is that many have written of late that Scripture and the Fathers of the Church are silent about the afterlife and reticent in their approach to this topic. Reticent they are, indeed, to speak of the mystical realm of Eternity in words that might make of Heaven the middle-class Protestant songfest so feared by Samuel Clemens, or cast Hell in images, not of metaphysical anguish, but of epic barbecues; but quiet about the afterlife Holy Scripture and the Fathers most certainly are not. Only our departure from Patristic study and from theology which derives from the Patristic mind can account for this great error among our contemporary theologians.

To return to a Patristic view of any religious subject is difficult. If dilettantism (not to mention mediocrity) and disbelief have become a hallmark of much of today's vogue and official theology, it is as much an optic as a scholarly disease: it distorts the vision of all those afflicted, such that they see, read, and perceive all that about them as accordingly superficial. Thus it is that in an evaluation in response to a request for funding, I recently found a polemical writer reacting to a collection of scholarly papers, based on years of meticulous study and Patristic exegesis, as mere "sermonettes." Many scholars have come to lack even the basic experience in research by which they might identify the authentic. Thus it is that I wish to preface the present little book with a warning to the dilettante and to the amateur scholar. There are here no inadequacies. There is here no modern scholar. In this little work by Professor Cavarnos, we find a study as studies should be: work drawn from the Fathers, scholarship shaped by the Patristic mind, and commentaries richly adorned with Patristic references.

Dr. Cavarnos exhibits in his writing the tell-tale sign of a good Patristic scholar: it is abundantly evident in his rich use of citations from primary sources that he *reads* the Fathers and reads them thoroughly. Trained in philosophy, he organizes, explains, and juxtaposes his primary citations in such a way as to present the Patristic witness with great clarity. He derives from the Fathers that catholicity in thought which makes them speak as from one mouth and as with one voice. To the proud dilettantes, who can but expound on what they do not adequately know, Cavarnos is a formidable challenger. His writing does not contain the pride which is necessary to their kind of theology; nor, to be sure, do their writings admit of the humility of a scholar who uses his talents to *present* and *offer* the words of the Fathers, rather than juggle them in a game of philosophical and theological prestidigitation.

If we have been heavy-handed and a bit harsh in dealing with much modern theological thought, it has been for the purpose of focusing the reader's attention on the unique scholarship which we find in this little book on the afterlife. After all, such scholarship really is threatened —it really is increasingly rare. Increasingly rare, too, as we have said, are those who can even recognize, today, an authentic piece of Patristic scholarship. In such circumstances, we are obliged to be blunt, to be strong in our statements, and perhaps to be at times hyperbolic in our expression —not in the interest of polemics, but as a device for commanding the attention of a Christian world which is being lulled into a harmful spiritual stupor.

There is a special quality in Professor Cavarnos' writings, beyond that of authenticity, which in turn challenges the modern believer, or demi-believer, as we have suggested. Our recognition of this quality is no personal laudation of the author as such, for it issues forth from the power of his sources themselves. From the Patristic and Scriptural references which Cavarnos has collected with such assiduity, there flows forth that "theology of facts" that so vibrantly enlivened the writings of the early Christian Fathers. If one rises above the merely scholarly and its aforementioned limitations, he senses —as if with some hidden intuitive faculty— that what he is reading of the afterlife is not the result of frivolous speculation or personal presumption, but just what it is: a description rendered by those who saw, and then wrote about, the life after death. This quality permeates Professor Cavarnos' writings. It is a quality bestowed upon any writings that authentically reflect the Patristic experience. And it is a quality which deeply affects the modern doubter or demi-believer.

It is a particular personal privilege to publish this book under the aegis of our monastery's publication program, which, though only several years old, has produced some six titles (four independently and two in conjunction with the Holy Cross Orthodox Press in Brookline, Massachusetts) of some popularity. In my own scholarly career, there have been several people who deeply affected me with the breadth of their scholarship and intellects. In the area of history and religious thought, two among those still living stand out particularly in my mind: Professor Cavarnos and the renowned Church historian and medievalist, Professor Jeffrey Russell of the University of California. The latter was a mentor; the former was not. But both have given me a vision of honest scholarship which has been sustained in contemporary times. At a time when belief in God is waning, Professor Russell has produced an exhaustive study of the devil that has received attention even in the popular press. His study of the devil has led many back to an understanding of God; for, what more quickly leads one to God than a belief in the existence of the devil? Dr. Cavarnos has likewise kept alive an understanding of the Byzantine mind and Orthodox spirituality that is almost gone in our dark days. In both of these men one finds that light which shines in darkness and a vision of true scholarship anchored in the enlightenment of the Christian Fathers and an inner knowledge of Jesus Christ.

Dr. Cavarnos has supplied us with much Patristic and Scriptural material not found in his original Greek edition of this book. We are very happy to add this material, which eloquently expands on the various themes put forth in the work. For any inadequacies in our publication, we take full responsibility, assuring the reader again that these are not the fault of the author, as his fine work will immediately make apparent to the reader. To the extent, then, that our own shortcomings will be readily visible, we apologize to the reader and ask for the author's forbearance.

Archimandrite Chrysostomos

PREFACE

The occasion for the writing of the present work was an invitation from the St. Andrew New England Clergy Brotherhood to speak on the subject of life after death. Responding to this invitation, I wrote a study, "The Future Life According to Orthodox Teaching." I presented this study to the numerous members of the Brotherhood on January 28, 1982, at the Diocesan House in Boston, in the presence of the [former] Bishop of Boston, His Grace, the Rt. Rev. Anthimos. The lively interest in the subject- matter of my talk by those present, as well as their expressed desire that I should publish my observations, prompted me to return to the text of the speech, enrich it, and improve its style. And so, with these finishing touches, it is published as the first chapter of this booklet.

While I was applying the finishing touches to my text, the thought occurred to me that it would be good to add, as supplements and as additional confirmations of all that I had presented in my talk on the future life, separate sections containing passages pertinent to this subject —selections from the Holy Scriptures, from the writings of the God-bearing Fathers, and from the Teachers and Hymnographers of the Orthodox Church.

I owe a warm debt of gratitude to the members of the St. Andrew Clergy Brotherhood for the honor paid me by the invitation to address them, for their cordial reception of my speech, and for their having incited me to release the material for publication. In particular, I must thank the President of the Brotherhood, Father George K. Papademetriou, for his repeatedly-expressed interest in the study, "The Future Life According to Orthodox Teaching," and his persistent exhortation that I prepare it for publication.

Constantine P. Cavarnos

I

THE FUTURE LIFE ACCORDING
TO ORTHODOX TEACHING

The subject of life after death is for every thinking man the most vital subject of all. During the modern epoch, however, with the secularization of religion and its relegation to the fringes of daily life, the subject has been swept away from the center of interest. Strangely, however, during the last few years there has been a noticeable rekindling of interest in life after death, indeed among scientists and, particularly, physicians. I might offer Drs. Elisabeth Kübler-Ross and Raymond Moody as examples. Kübler-Ross has given lectures on this subject that have made her internationally known. Among her lectures is one entitled, "Death Does Not Exist."[1] Moody has written two books related to the subject of life after death: *Life after Life* and *Reflections on Life after Life.* The first was published in 1975, the second in 1977.[2] They have been repeatedly reprinted and have sold millions of copies.

A rekindling of interest in life after death can also be observed among Orthodox Christians. For example, the book Σημεῖον Μέγα [*A Great Sign*] by the blessed Photios Kontoglou, first published in 1962, essentially deals with the subject of the other life. It is distinguished by its having the largest circulation of any of his books. Another Orthodox writer, Hieromonk Seraphim (Rose), a convert to Orthodoxy, wrote a book entitled, *The Soul After Death.*[3] In this work, published in 1980, the traditional Orthodox teaching on the subject is set forth and, with that teaching as a base, contemporary "after-death" and "out-of-the-body" experiences are interpreted.

The occasion for interest in the subject of life after death among those working within the discipline of medical science stems, above all, from the fact that progress in medical technology in recent years has given physicians the capability of bringing back to life people who had been declared dead and who were, in keeping with the criteria of science, considered dead, if for seconds[4] or even for hours.[5] They were "clinically dead," as this condition is called. A person is "clinically dead" when his breathing and heart have stopped for an ex-extended period of time, when his blood pressure has fallen so much that the sphygmomanometer registers "zero," when the pupils of his eyes have dilated, his body temperature has begun to fall, and so forth. This is the clinical definition —which is signified by the phrase, "so-and-so died." This definition "has been employed for centuries, both by doctors and laymen."[6] The ways by which, in certain cases, medical science brings people clinically dead back to life are the injection of adrenalin into the heart, the utilization of machines that stimulate the heart to work, the use of mechanical hearts or lungs, and other such means.[7] Another important reason for the rekindling of interest in life after death among physicians is a change in their mentality. Until recently, it was considered inappropriate for a doctor to give public attention to this subject, to lecture on it, or to write about it. Those who did not conform to this mentality were in jeopardy of losing respect among their colleagues. Today, this danger has almost completely disappeared. All a doctor need do is exercise caution, formulating his views objectively and, in general, in a scientific fashion.

Religious interest in the subject of life after death has been aroused, on the one hand, by the publications and lectures of scientists, such as those whom we have mentioned, and, on the other hand, by supernatural events of recent times, such as those related by Kontoglou in his book, *A Great Sign*. In his book, the ever memorable Photios gives detailed descriptions of the numerous appearances of the Holy Martyrs Raphael, Nicholas, and Irene, who died 500 years ago at Thermes, on the island of Lesvos. This multitude of astonishing appearances by the spirits of people who have died —indeed, Saints— can be explained as a clear manifestation of Divine Grace. Seeing man's unprecedented disbelief in life beyond the grave, God, being compassionate and a lover of mankind, wanted to lead man, by means of these numerous appearances, to faith in the eternal life in Christ. This explanation is in agreement with the saying of the Apostle Paul: "Where sin abounded, grace did much more abound: that as sin hath reigned unto death, even so might grace reign through righteousness unto eternal life by Jesus Christ."[8] Through such supernatural events, people are led from disbelief to belief. For, as St. Gregory the Theologian observes, "miracles are for unbelievers," that they might believe.

Insofar as the aim of my talk is to give a general view of the teaching of the Orthodox Church on the subject of life after death, I will not deal with the conclusions of contemporary physicians, who have conducted specific investigations with regard to the same. I will simply note that their investigations constitute a confirmation of Orthodox teaching on the following points: 1) that death does not constitute an annihilation of the human person, since, besides the visible man, the body, there is the invisible man, the soul, which continues to exist beyond death; 2) that the soul, separated from the body, maintains self-consciousness and does not fall into a state of sleep or unconsciousness; 3) that the soul, separated from and outside the body, continues to think —and, in fact, clearly —, to have feelings, such as fear and serenity, sorrow and joy, etc.; 4) that after death the soul maintains its memory intact, remembering all of its deeds, all thoughts, all the words it spoke, and so on, from its childhood years forth; 5) that the soul has senses that correspond to the bodily senses of sight and hearing, so that, separated from the body, it can see and hear. These are all testified to by a multitude of people who, according to the criteria of medical science, were dead for a certain period of time. These people all have experienced the departure of their souls —their spirits— from their bodies, finding themselves some distance from their bodies. By means of the current medical technology used for resuscitation, their bodies were revived, their souls returned to them.

These data from physicians conducting research in the field constitute, in our time, a significant verification of Orthodox teaching. With regard to the full truth about the future life, nonetheless, they are not enough to satisfy the human heart, which thirsts for Eternity. They are restricted to events that befall the human being for a brief period of time after the experience of death, whereas the real concern of man is one of learning what happens in time ever-lasting: whether or not the soul maintains its existence eternally —that is, whether or not the soul is immortal. Moreover, we would like to learn what the best preparation for eternal life is in our life here. And the Christian is not only concerned about the continuation of his spiritual existence beyond the grave, but also about the resurrection of the body: he looks for the resurrection of the dead. Medical science is by nature incapable of giving answers to these questions. The method it uses, as much as the aims it pursues, preclude its ability to reply to these questions. For example, the aim of medical science is the restoration and maintenance of the body's health, not the solution of metaphysical and ethical problems, such as questions about eternal life and salvation. Here, then, religion enters, its main purpose being preoccupation with such problems.

The Orthodox Church has a full and very precise teaching on the questions of the constitution of man, the

nature of the soul, the relationship between the body and
the soul, the nature of death, Paradise and Hell, and the
general destiny of man. This teaching is contained in the
Holy Scriptures, in the writings of the God-bearing Fathers and Teachers of the Church —most notably in
the writings of the ascetics and mystics—, in the lives
of the Saints, and in the Church's Hymnography and
Iconography.

According to Orthodox anthropology, man has a
two-fold nature, consisting of a material, visible body,
which is called the "outer man," and an immaterial,
invisible soul, which is called the "inner man." Christ
alludes to this dual composition when He says: "Take
no thought for your life [τῇ ψυχῇ, literally, *for your
soul*], what ye shall eat, or what ye shall drink; nor yet
for your body, what ye shall put on. Is not the life more
than meat, and the body than raiment?"[9] The blessed Apostle Paul declares this, saying, "Though our
outward man perish, yet the inner man is renewed day
by day."[10] The Holy Fathers frequently refer to this
dual composition. For example, the divine Gregory of
Nyssa notes, "For there are two beings from which man
has been put together —one spiritual, the other bodily—,
the outer one containing the inner one, and the inner
one, during this lifetime, dwelling in the outer one."[11]
St. Symeon the New Theologian, the great mystical
Father, writes: "Of all visible and invisible beings, only
man was created by God as a double creature, having a
body comprised of the four elements, sensation, and
breath, and a spiritual, immaterial, and bodiless soul inexpressibly and in an unfathomable way united to the
body; these constitute the man —a mortal and immortal
creature, visible and invisible, sensible and intelligible.[12]

Of these two components of man, body and soul,
the soul is incomparably more important and superior.
Jesus taught this when, for example, he said: "For what
is a man profited, if he shall gain the whole world, and
lose his own soul? Or what shall a man give in exchange

for his soul?"[13] Speaking of this supremacy of the soul, and equating the soul with the self, the man proper, St. Basil the Great notes: "The self is the inner man. The outer parts are not the self, but belongings of it. For the self is not the hand, but rather the rational faculty of the soul, while the hand is a part of man. Thus while the body is an instrument of man, an instrument of the soul, man, strictly speaking, is chiefly the soul."[14] Similarly, St. Nikodemos the Hagiorite says: "Your true self —that which is the man proper— is not the visible body..., but the inner being, the spiritual man; for it is the soul that vivifies, nurtures, and makes the body to move and to sense. Without the soul, the body is dead, motionless, and senseless."[15]

These two existent things, as the Fathers call them, the soul and the body, are "inexpressibly and inscrutably" united, the one influencing the other. "There is an interaction and reciprocity between the soul and the body, the soul acting on the body and, conversely, the body on the soul, ...and the one communicates its peculiar traits to the other," the divine Nikodemos observes, summarizing the teaching of the Fathers. He goes on to say that all of this takes place, "as a result of the ineffable bond between the body and the soul, even though exactly how this happens, and why, is something hidden to all philosophers and theologians alike."[16]

The soul gives life to the body, holds it together, and rules it. "By nature, the soul vivifies the body," St. Thalassios writes. [17] "The soul holds the body together," observes St. Symeon the New Theologian, "binding together all of its members by its own particular power and keeping them all well united with much concord, so that each member is aided by the other; by the bond of the soul alone they are controlled and secured."[18] Likewise, St. Ephraim the Syrian writes: "The soul acts on all [the members of the body], for it rules the body; it gives life to the flesh...."[19]

We have observed that the soul and body have a

mutual influence on one another and the manner in which the soul influences the body. But how does the body act upon the soul? By communicating something of its own state to the soul. For example, when the body is ill, the soul also suffers. St. Isaac the Syrian, in referring to this matter, notes: "The soul groans along with the body at the amputation of one of its limbs, in fevers, in illnesses, and in similar matters. For in its union with the body, the soul suffers along with it, just as the body also suffers along with the soul, is moved by the joy of the soul, and participates in its afflictions."[20]

Despite the soul's bond to the body and the body's influence on the soul, the soul is essentially independent from the body. Its existence does not depend on the body, while the body, separated from the soul, dies, since, as we have seen, the soul is that which gives life to the body, holds it together, and rules.

However, the bond which unites the soul to the body is difficult to dissolve. The dissolution of this bond is called death. As we have noted, mainstream medical science, engrossed with the outer man (the body), identifies death with various phenomena that relate exclusively to the body. It defines death by referring to such phenomena as the cessation of the heartbeat and breathing, the disappearance of blood pressure, the cooling of the body, and other similar phenomena. Our religion, having not only the outer, but also the inner, man in view, defines death in a far profounder and more essential way. The Patristic texts characterize death as an "exodus," "unloosing," and "separation." They characterize death as an exodus because it entails the departure of the soul from the body and from the visible world in general. The word "exodus" with this connotation is found both in the Old and New Testaments.[21] Likewise, the word "unloosing" is found in the Holy Scriptures.[22] It, like the word "exodus," also implies two things. On the one hand, it alludes to the loosing of the bond that unites the soul with the body, and, on the other, to the soul's going from the visible, material world —to which the body belongs— to the invisible, spiritual world. In Patristic texts and Church Hymnography, this going over is also called a departure. In keeping with this terminology, the deceased is characterized as "departed," since his soul, which chiefly constitutes man, has departed, going over to the next world from this one. The notion of death as a "separation" of the soul from the body finds poetic expression in the *idiomelon* for the dead in the fourth tone, the work of St. John Damascene. This *idiomelon* reads:

Truly most frightening is the mystery of death, how the soul is violently *separated* from its concord with the body and, by divine decree, the most natural bond of their cohesion is severed. Wherefore, we implore Thee, O Giver of Life Who lovest mankind, to grant rest to the [newly] departed one in the dwellings of the righteous.

This *troparion* is also interesting because of its use of two previously cited terms: "bond" and "departed." The term "separation," like the other two terms used in reference to death, also has a dual meaning. On the one hand, it alludes to the separation of the soul from the body, and, on the other, to the soul's separation from the material world. One Patristic text speaks as follows about this two-fold separation: "Blessed is he who finds confidence in the hour of his separation from the world, when the soul parts [is separated] in fear and suffering; for the angels come to take the soul and separate it from the body."[23]

The separation of the soul from the body is performed by an Angel of God, not only in the case of the righteous, but of sinners also. "Neither are the souls of sinners separated without an Angel," says Saint Symeon the Archbishop of Thessalonica, "that the wretched

Enemy (i.e., the Devil) should find no time or place to bring death to a man, lest, in the course of time, he might come to be reckoned the master of life and death."[24] The separation takes place after the command from God, as the following hymn, chanted at the Vespers of Friday of the Plagal of the First Tone, says:

O Christ, spare me, Thy servant, when my soul is to be separated from the body *at the command given by Thee,* Who didst unite into one dust and spirit by divine beckoning; spare me from the assault and ill-treatment of invisible enemies that lie in wait to wrench me away mercilessly....[25]

At the time of separation, the soul sees ".all the works it performed, good and bad, by day and by night," as St. Ephraim the Syrian writes. "The sinner's soul parts from the body in fear and, trembling, it sets off to be present at the Immortal Tribunal."[26] Giving examples of men who are grieved at the hour of death, St. Ephraim writes: "Grieved is the presumptuous man; grieved the indifferent; grieved the lazy, who neglected to do what was pleasing to God; grieved is the man who has much property, who gave his soul for worldly things; grieved is the rich man, for he is separated from his riches.... All these are grieved at the hour of death, for they are given to things worldly."[27] On the other hand, the hour of the soul's separation from the body does not grieve the righteous; rather, it gives them joy. The same Saint writes the following related words: "The time of separation does not grieve him who frees himself from everything earthly.... The righteous, the holy, and the ascetics rejoice at the hour of death and separation, having the great labors of their asceticism, vigils and prayers, fasts and tears, sackcloth and the subjection of their bodies to hardship before their eyes. Their souls leap up, for they are prepared to go out of their bodies for their rest." [28]   Similarly, the celestial Seraphim of Sarov, once speaking of such souls, remarked: "What joy, what exultation await the soul when God's Angels come to take it."[29]

After the separation of the soul from the body, the "Particular Judgement" takes place, according to the words of the Apostle Paul: "It is appointed unto man once to die, but after this the judgement."[30] According to the following saying of Christ the Savior, those who do not attain to the perfection of the Saints come into judgement: "He that heareth my word, and believeth on him that sent me, hath everlasting life, and shall not come into condemnation [in the Greek, κρίσιν, or *judgement*]; but is passed from death unto life."[31] St. Maximos the Confessor says the following pertinent words: "Those who have acquired perfect love of God and have, through their virtues, risen on the wings of the soul, will 'be caught up in the clouds,' as the Apostle says, and will not be brought to judgement. On the other hand, those who have not acquired love in all its perfection, but have both sins and virtues on their account, will appear before the court of judgment. There they will be tried, as it were, by fire. Their good actions will be put in the balance against the bad, and if the good outweigh the bad, they will be delivered from punishment."[32]

The judgement that takes place in the case of the imperfect is termed a "calling to account" [or *cross-examination*] by St. John Klimakos[33] and other Fathers, as it is also in Church Hymnography. Thus the *prosomoion* to the *Theotokos* in the fourth tone sung at Tuesday evening Vespers, as appointed in the *Parakletike* [*Oktoechos*], begins with the following words:

O Bride of God, the most dreadful gloom of death torments my soul; thought of the demons' calling to account, O Good One, continually upsets my soul and makes me tremble....

The "calling to account" sometimes begins before death. For example, St. John Klimakos gives the following case in the seventh step of his *Ladder.* There was once a hermit named Stephan, who fell ill and, after a few days, reposed. A day before his death, "he went into mental ecstasy and, with his eyes open, looked to the right and left of his bed and, as if he were being called to account by someone, said, within earshot of all of the bystanders: 'Yes, indeed that is true; but that is why I fasted for so many years.' And then, 'No, actually you are lying; I did not do that.' And then again, 'Yes, it is true; but I wept and served the brethren.' Yet again, 'Yes, it is true. Yes, but I do not know what to say to this; in God there is mercy.' And it was an awful and horrible sight, this invisible and merciless calling to account. What was most terrible, moreover, was that he was accused even of what he had not done. And while being thus called to account, he was parted from his body, leaving us in uncertainty as to his judgement, or end, or sentence, or how the calling to account ended."[34]

This example helps us to understand what the calling to account is. It is the test to which the demons subject the imperfect soul. When such a soul is finally separated from the body, the Lord's Angels take hold of it to convey it to the Most Just Judge, Christ, to Whom, as we read in the Gospel, the Father has committed all judgment: "For the Father judgeth no man, but hath committed all judgment unto the Son."[35] Then the demons attempt to take the soul from the Angels, declaring that it belongs to them because it lived according to their desires. The threatening demons reproach the soul with various sins it committed, even slandering the soul with sins that it in fact did not commit.

There are numberless passages in the Fathers and in [Church] Hymnography that refer to the assault by the demons. I will give a few examples.

The Wakeful Father Abba Isaiah tells us: Live "every day having death before your eyes, and concerning yourselves with how you will come out from the body, how you will pass by the powers of darkness that will meet you in the air, and how you will answer before God...."[36]

"For when the soul comes out from the body, the Angels accompany it, and at that time all of the powers of darkness come out to meet it and, desiring to seize the soul, investigate whether there is anything of themselves in it."[37]

Another of the Wakeful Fathers, Diadochos of Photiki, says: "If we do not confess our involuntary sins as we should, we shall discover a certain timidity in ourselves at the hour of our death [exodus].... For if we are afraid then, we will not be able freely to pass by the rulers of the nether world. They will have as an advocate like themselves to plead against us the fear which our soul experiences because of its own wickedness. But the soul which rejoices in the love of God, at the hour of its departure, is lifted with the Angels of peace above all the hosts of darkness...."[38]

From Church Hymnography, I cite two *theotokia*:

When my soul is about to be separated violently from the members of the body, then, O Bride of God, come to my aid; scatter the counsels of the fleshless enemies and shatter their millstones, by which they seek to devour me mercilessly; that, unhindered, I may pass through the rulers of darkness standing in the air.[39]

At the hour of my passing, grant that without grief I may pass by the incorporeal satraps and the tyrannical battle-array in the air, that joyfully I may cry 'Rejoice' to Thee O Lady; Rejoice unashamed hope of all.[40]

During the attack of the demons, the soul defends itself, being aided by the Holy Angels, who report the soul's good deeds. As Abba Isaiah says, "at that time the Angels do not war with them [the demons] ; rather, the good deeds performed by the soul build a wall around it and protect it from them." [41]

Here the word "deeds" means not only external good deeds, such as almsgiving and visits to the sick, but also internal works, such as repentance, prayer, sobriety, and virtues in general. Emphasizing these internal works, St. Ephraim the Syrian says:

> No one will help us in that day —neither friend nor relation. Only our repentance in this world, with its accompanying virtues, namely true love, humility, obedience, and temperance will help us. These accompany us when we set off from this ephemeral world. They resist those opposing powers which wish to seize us.[42]

When the soul's works and virtues defeat the demons, then, as Abba Isaiah says, "the Angels sing before the soul until, with delight, it meets God."[43]

The souls of the sinners, those who die unrepentant, without works, without virtues to protect them from the opposing powers —these souls are seized by the demons. They are not taken, though, against God's consent and without a divine concession, for God is the Lord of life and death.[44]

Thus the calling to account ends either with the safe passage of the soul through the midst of the demons, or with its being handed over to them.

That the souls of the righteous are taken by the Angels, while the souls of the sinners are seized by demons, is something which has been made known to us, St. Symeon of Thessalonica says, "from many stories and discourses of the Fathers. And the Holy Gospel says this with regard to poor Lazarus, who, on dying, was taken to the bosom of Abraham by the Angels.[45] The [departing] souls seen by the divine Anthony, as related by St. Athanasios the Great in his life of St. Anthony, also bear witness this: that of Ammoun of Nitria and that of Paul of Thebes. The blessed souls of many other Saints also testify to this."[46] With regard to seeing St. Ammoun's soul, Athanasios the Great says that Anthony the Great was once on the mountain, sitting and looking up. He saw that someone was being borne upward into the air and that there was great rejoicing among those who were meeting him. Then, admiring and blessing this chorus, he prayed that he might learn who it was. And he immediately heard a voice telling him that this was the soul of Ammoun, a solitary in Nitria. Ammoun abode there as an ascetic until his old age. It was a thirty-day journey from Nitria to the mountain where St. Anthony lived. The monks to whom he told of the death of Ammoun noted the day. And when, after thirty days, certain brothers arrived from Nitria, they inquired and learned that Ammoun had died exactly the day and hour that Anthony the Great saw Ammoun's soul being taken up by the Angels.[47]

In Byzantine Iconography, there is an Icon that bears the inscription: "St. Anthony sees the soul of Abba Ammoun." A mountain is depicted on this Icon. St. Anthony is standing on the mountain, watching the soul of Ammoun ascend, carried by Angels.[48] In Icons, the soul is depicted with the form of the body, as in the Icon of the Dormition of the *Theotokos* (where we see Christ holding the soul of the *Theotokos*). This is because the departing soul appears in this form to spiritual vision. Moreover, according to the divine Makarios of Egypt, the soul really does have the form of the outer man. He says that just as the outer man, that is, the body, has a form, so the inner man has a form that resembles the outer man.[49] The fact that the soul is spiritual, incorporeal does not constitute a contradiction to this. As St. John Damascene notes, "for everything compared with God, Who alone is incomparable, is found to be gross and material. For in reality only the Deity is immaterial and incorporeal."[50] Also, the soul (that has separated from the body) is depicted at an infant's age to symbolize the beginning of a new stage of life after death.

With regard to the number of Angels that receive the souls of the righteous, St. Symeon of Thessalonica

makes the following observation: "In the sayings of the
Fathers we find that often one Angel, ...but also often
two or more Angels, come to take a soul. So there
is a certain fixed number of angels for this work.
But I think that the number is according to the
worthiness of the souls...."[51] From visions such as that
of St. Anthony the Great, we know, adds Symeon, that
the blessed souls of the Saints are escorted and ac-
companied to the place appointed them by God not only by Angels, but by Saints also. The Saints are sent by
God "for consolation and honor."[52] A vision by St. Anthony bears witness to one such case. In the *Evergetinos*, we read of the following event:

> St. Anthony was coming back to St. Paul of Thebes,
> to whom, according to the instructions he had re-
> ceived from St. Athanasios, he was bringing the
> cloak of the latter. As he was approaching the cave
> [where he had left St. Paul], at about the third
> hour of the day (9 a.m.), he saw, with the eyes
> of his soul —with which only the worthy can see—
> orders of Angels, groups of Apostles, choirs of
> Prophets, and ranks of Martyrs. And in the midst
> of this holy array he saw Paul's soul, exceeding
> in brightness the white of snow, shining more
> brilliantly than the snow, and with great joy ascend-
> ing to Heaven.[53]

A vision of St. Paphnutios, which he saw one day
before his death, constitutes a similar case. In the same
book [the *Evergetinos*], we read the following:

> The great Paphnutios grew to extreme old age. And
> he was, from the great measure of his asceticism
> and hardship, as one without flesh. Then an Angel
> of the Lord came from Heaven and said to Paphnu-
> tios: 'O blessed one, the Lord calls you to the eter-
> nal mansions. To honor you, therefore, the Pro-
> phets and the righteous have come to accompany

you to the dwelling place of God.' Our holy Father Paphnutios lived only one more day after the appearance of the Angel, during which time a multitude of Elders and Priests came for his divinely-revealed repose, for the Saint foretold to them that on that day he was to take leave of the present life. Then he gave up his soul, wholly illuminated, into the hands of God, and the holy Elders saw it clearly enrolled among the choirs of the righteous, and they glorified God.[54]

The souls of those who have lived in a virtuous and God-pleasing manner are led by the Angels to those abodes of the spiritual universe that are worthy of the way of life and character of such souls, namely, to places of light and places of joy, where God, the orders of Angels, and the choirs of Saints abide. These places are collectively referred to as the Spiritual Paradise. But the souls of sinners are taken to Hades, to the place of Partial Damnation, to places of darkness and sorrow, where the Devil —the Prince of evil—, the demons, and all kinds of sinners dwell.

Where each soul that has finally been separated from the body will be led is determined neither by the demons nor by Angels, but by God, the omniscient and righteous judge. He pronounces the verdict and, in keeping with this, the soul is led either to Paradise or to Hell. This judgment of God is called the "Particular Judgment."

In regard to the entire theme of the calling to account and the Particular Judgment, blessed Archbishop Theophilos[55] writes:

"When the soul is parting from the body, or afterwards, when it has fully parted, ...all the leaders and powers of darkness overtake the soul and present to it all the sins it committed, whether in knowledge or ignorance, from the time the person was born until his last hour, when the soul was separated from the body.

These powers stand near the soul shamelessly and accuse it with vehemence. Face to face with these hostile powers of darkness stand the holy powers, the Angels, revealing and citing all the good works which the soul happened to have performed. What agony and terror, then, do you think the soul will experience when it finds itself before such an examination, facing such a frightening and unbribable tribunal, ...until the verdict of the tribunal be given and the soul be delivered from those that hinder it? This very hour is the moment of the soul's greatest trial, until its judgment is finished and it hears the judgment of the Righteous Judge.

"And so, if by the verdict of the Righteous Judge the soul be given freedom, then immediately the enemies are put to shame, the luminous Angels seize the soul from them, and with no further obstructions it is led by the Angels to that unutterable joy and glory, to which it will finally be established. If, however, the soul lived carelessly and so was found unworthy of freedom, then it will hear that most terrifying voice: 'Take this ungodly one away from here, that he see not the glory of the Lord' (Isaiah 26:10)."[56]

The soul now enters into what is called the "Middle State." Here it will remain until the Great Judgment. In the Middle State, souls do not have the full retribution either for virtue or vice. Concerning this state, St. Nektarios of Aegina says:

"In this state the souls of the righteous have a foretaste of the blessedness prepared for them, while the sinners experience to a certain extent the eternal and complete suffering that awaits them.... The righteous in Heaven and the sinners in Hades have only a foretaste of the blessedness or suffering which they deserve."[57]

Complete blessedness and complete torment are states that will occur after the Second Coming of Christ and after what is called the General Judgment. As the God-inspired Symeon the New Theologian remarks, when the righteous "die, they do not descend to

Hades, but they ascend to Heaven. And there they are deemed worthy to obtain the delight that is found in that place, and everlasting joy. Now this enjoyment is only in part; after the General Resurrection of the dead, it will be in full." But when sinners who did not participate in Christ, or who dishonored participating in Christ by a life contrary thereto, die, they descend to Hades, and after the General Resurrection there awaits them "another death, much more grievous and bitter than the one occurring now, that of eternal torment."[58]

In the Middle State, souls maintain their memory and self-consciousness intact, thinking and feeling, indeed, more clearly than in this world. About this, Abba Dorotheos says:

"As the Fathers say, the soul remembers everything that it did here —words, deeds, and thoughts— and none of these can be forgotten.... Whatever good or evil it did, it remembers, and none of this is lost. And if a soul benefited someone or was benefited by someone else, it remembers him whom it benefited or by whom it was benefited. Likewise, if it was injured by someone or injured someone else, it remembers this also. As I said, the soul forgets nothing that it did in this world, but remembers it all when it comes out from the body; —to be sure, it remembers more things, and it remembers more clearly, being delivered from this earthly body."[59]

The story of the rich man and poor Lazarus, related by the Lord, also teaches that the memory is preserved after death:

"And it came to pass, that the beggar [Lazarus] died, and was carried by the angels into Abraham's bosom: the rich man also died, and was buried; and in hell he lift up his eyes, being in torments, and seeth Abraham afar off, and Lazarus in his bosom. And he cried and said, Father Abraham, have mercy on me, and send Lazarus, that he might dip the tip of his finger in water and cool my tongue; for I am tormented in this flame. But Abraham said, Son, remember that thou in thy lifetime receivedst thy good things, and likewise Lazarus evil things: but now he is comforted, and thou art tormented...."[60] The rich man remembers Lazarus and Abraham tells the rich man to recall the enjoyable life he lived in this world and, in contrast, the evil that Lazarus suffered. Continuing, the rich man remembers his five brothers who are still alive, and he asks Abraham to send Lazarus to admonish them, that they might not also come "into this place of torment."[61] From this story we learn that not only the memory is preserved after death, but also the powers of feeling and reflection: the rich man —his spirit— suffers in his place in Hell and thinks about how, if possible, he might relieve his pain and aid his brothers.

The following passage by the theologian Chrestos Androutsos constitutes an excellent summary of what has been said so far with regard to the Middle State:

"The souls in the middle state..., though bodiless, have self-consciousness and consequently feel, comprehend, and, in general, exercise all of the powers of the soul. The term *sleeping* that is used to characterize death refers to the body, not to the soul."[62]

An important element of Orthodox teaching on the Middle State is the fact that the souls of the righteous know each other. In keeping with this, St. Athanasios the Great writes:

"God has granted those who are saved the ability, until the general resurrection, to meet and rejoice with one another, having the expectation of the future divine gifts that will be conferred upon them."[63]

In a revealing homily of St. Makarios of Egypt, we read:

"In that world... men recognize one another, and rejoice and converse with one another, just as some do here in the market place. There also, one sees men of nobility and poverty, and he asks, 'Who is this?' and 'Who is that?' And by his questions he learns even of those whom he has not known. Thus it is in that world. But I speak of the righteous; the sinners are deprived of this."[64]

It should also be added, with regard to the Middle State, that both Paradise (the Bosom of Abraham, the Kingdom of God, the Kingdom of Heaven) and Hell (Gehenna, Hades) have levels. The same Makarios says of this:

"Some say that there is one kingdom and one hell; but we say that there are many levels and differences and measures, both in the kingdom and in hell.... The Godhead looks upon men, providentially ordering all things according to reason.... God, being a just judge, gives to each a reward according to the measure of faith.... For there are superior measures, and there are little measures, and in light and glory there are differences, and in hell itself appear magicians and robbers, as well as others who have committed only little sins. Those who say that there is one kingdom and one hell, and that there are no levels, say ill."[65]

Likewise, the divine Gregory of Sinai says:

"The differing degrees of ascent and advancement in the state of souls in heaven are called 'many mansions' by the Savior. The kingdom is one, but there are many distinctions within it —for so it is with things of heaven and earth—, according to both virtue and knowledge, and also according to the degree of the soul's deification. For, 'there is one glory of the sun, and another of the moon, and another glory of the stars; and one star differeth from another star in glory,' as the Apostle says, though all shine in one firmament.... Hells also differ.... But they are all within Hades, according to Scripture, which says: 'to a land of darkness and gloominess, to a land of perpetual darkness,' where sinners dwell before the [General] Judgment, and where they return after the verdict." [66]

Speaking in detail about the different hells, St. Ephraim the Syrian observes:

"There is an outer darkness, as we hear in the Gospel, and consequently there is an inner one. The Gehenna of fire is one place; the gnashing of teeth, the unsleeping worm, the lake of fire, the inextinguishable fire, and the fiery river are others. The miserable sinners are distributed among these hells, each one according to his sins. And as there are different sins, so also are there different hells. Thus, there is one kind of hell for the adulterer, another for the fornicator, another for the murderer, and another for the thief and the drunkard...."[67]

Nowadays, many who speak about Paradise and Hell avoid the term "place." They say that Paradise and Hell are simply "states" of the soul and not "places." But the fact is that not only the Fathers, but also the Hymnographers of the Church, refer to *both* Paradise and Hell as places, and the God-Man Himself speaks of a place in Heaven and Hell. In the fourteenth chapter of the Gospel of St. John, Christ says: "In my Father's house are many mansions: if it were not so, I would have told you. I go to prepare a place for you. And if I go and prepare a place for you, I will come again, and receive you unto myself; that where I am, there ye may be also."[68] In the sixteenth chapter of the Gospel of St. Luke, he refers to Hell, where the soul of the rich man has gone, as a "place of torment."[69] With regard to Church Hymnography, I will cite the *prokeimenon* sung at the Funeral Service as an example:

Blessed is the way wherein you proceed today, for there is prepared for you a place of rest.

And I will add that in this same Service the priest says aloud: "O lord, give rest to thy departed servant in a place of light, in a verdant place, from whence pain, sorrow, and sighing are fled away." As regards the God-bearing Fathers, I will note that we can see their characteristic manner of speaking of Paradise and Hell as "places" in the following passage from Abba Dorotheos:

"The saints are received into certain places of light and angelic happiness, but sinners are received into places of darkness, full of fear and trembling, as the saints tell us."[70]

"Space" in the spiritual world, where souls go and abide after death, is not the same as space in the physical world, where material bodies exist and move about; it is different from this. Likewise, "time" in the spiritual world is of a different nature than time in the material world, the time that is measured by watches.[71]

In regard to the possibility of a change in the soul's condition during the interval between the Particular and General Judgements, the Orthodox Church teaches that it is possible for it to change for the better. The God-enlightened John the Damascene emphasizes this in his treatise, *Concerning the Departed Faithful: That the Liturgies and Charities Performed for Them are to Their Benefit.* He observes how the divine Apostles decreed that "at the dread and immaculate and life-giving mysteries" those who had faithfully departed were to be commemorated and that since then the Orthodox Church has practiced this everywhere, and will continue to practice it until the end of the world. He notes that the commemoration brings them much gain and benefit. He adds that benevolences performed for the poor on behalf of the dead benefit the latter greatly, as also does the lighting of sacred lamps and candles in their memory. In his own words, this divine Father says:

"Do not reject bringing oil for the sacred lamp at the tomb and lighting candles there when entreating Christ God, for these are acceptable to God and bring a great return. For the oil and wax are the sacrifice of a burnt offering; the bloodless sacrifice is an expiation; and benevolences extended to the poor are an addition to every good return."[72]

The ecclesiastical writer Damaskinos the Studite, who flourished in the sixteenth century, speaks in a similar manner. In his work *Treasury*, which was very widely read for whole centuries, we read:

"If you want to benefit the departed, practice charity on their behalf; give to the poor, the orphans, the strangers, the imprisoned, and to the priests also, that in the church they might pray for them and commemorate them. If you want to do what is good for the departed, keep his (memorial on the) third day, the ninth day, the fortieth day, at one year, and at all that follow. Have as many liturgies as you can.... If you can, light a candle at his grave and keep the lamp burning there on sacred feasts and on Sundays.... And, blessed Christians, as many of you as have heard what the works of Christian order are, practice them, that our Lord Jesus Christ might grant rest to the soul of the departed in the bosom of Abraham and in His Kingdom."[73]

In recent times, the possibility of the improvement of the departed's condition has been especially emphasized by St. Nectarios of Aegina in his book, *Study Concerning the Immortality of the Soul and the Holy Memorial Services.* In this work he has brought together a multitude of related passages from the writings of the Holy Fathers and has drawn on the testimony of the divine Liturgies and the Diptychs of the Church. In this Middle State, says the blessed Nectarios, "some of the sinners will be relieved of the burden of the penalty and will be completely delivered from sufferings of Hades, not through their own action," not through some Purgatorial Fire as Roman Catholicism teaches "but through the prayers of the Church."[74] By the prayers of the Church he particularly means the holy Memorial Services. Regarding the value of the Memorial Services, he writes the following important words:

"The Church believes: that the supplications and entreaties She makes for Her children are heard by our man-loving Saviour, and that She occasions a forgiving of sins for those for whom the Memorial Services are held; that the final verdict with regard to reward and punishment has not been pronounced; that this verdict is reserved for the Second and dread Coming of the Master Christ; and that until the Second Coming of Christ the Church can offer up to the Lord prayers and supplications for Her children."[75]

St. Nectarios explains that the Church performs these duties "for Her faithful and pious children who have reposed in full communion with the precious Body and Blood of Christ the Saviour."[76] She prays that God, "Who is good and loves mankind, might forgive these trespasses of Her children who have reposed in the Lord, pardon their sins, whether in word, deed, or thought, . . . establish their souls where the just repose, and make them heirs of His heavenly kingdom. . . . As co-supplicants on behalf of the departed before the Lord, She brings forward the Saints, the Prophets, the Apostles, the Martyrs, the Confessors . . . , for 'the effectual fervent prayer of a righteous man availeth much' (St. James 5:16), and, above all, the most holy Virgin Theotokos. . . ."[77] In doing this, "the Church does not promise their inevitable salvation; this would be an improper claim."[78] But She hopes in God's "love of man, mercy, benevolence, and affection."[79] And for those "who lived impiously and came to an evil end, She does not pray that God will establish their souls where the just repose, but that He will lighten their torments."[80]

Besides the holy Memorial Services, Saint Nectarios mentions prayers in general and almsgiving performed for the dead. After death, the soul cannot perform salutary works that would deliver it from Hades. But the "divine Liturgies and the prayers performed by the righteous and by those who knew the departed, as well as the giving of alms, become causes for salvation and liberation from Hades."[81]

The teaching of the Church on the subject of the Middle State is confirmed by the experience of Her children, and by those who have progressed spiritually. Referring to his personal experience, but out of humility presenting it as the experience of someone else, the Apostle Paul writes in the Second Epistle to the Corinthians:

"I knew a man in Christ above fourteen years ago, (whether in the body, I cannot tell; or whether out of the body, I cannot tell: God knoweth;) such an one caught up to the third heaven. And I knew such a man, (whether in the body, or out of the body, I cannot tell: God knoweth;) how that he was caught up into paradise, and heard unspeakable words, which it is not lawful for a man to utter."[82]

Dwelling at greater length on this kind of experience, Athanasios the Great writes:

"All those who have their mind on high, all those who forget the things of the earth, all those who give no care to the flesh, ... who, to be sure, have mortified their earthly members, having a pure mind and an acute mind's eye, being yet on earth these see the sufferings that are in hell, the eternal torments, the everlasting fire, the outer darkness, the weeping and the gnashing of teeth. But they also see the heavenly gifts that God has presented to the Saints: the royal attire, the shining inner chambers, the inexpressible delights and eternal life. What more can I say? Indeed the greatest wonder of all is that he who has a pure mind also perceives with his inner eyes even God Himself."[83]

With the following words, St. Symeon the New Theologian gives a first-hand account of an "out of the body" experience of Heaven and subsequent return to the body:

"I was wholly cast out (of the body), and lost power over it.... Ah me! How shall I ever describe this adequately! What love, what goodness! He leads me out of Hell, out of that place and its darkness, and leads me into another world, or up in the air someplace. I really am not able to say which. This I know, that it is a light and that it carries me and sustains me and leads me toward a great light. This great divine marvel, not even angels could describe or speak about among themselves, at all, or so it seems to me. After I arrived there, he shows me still other things, those things found in the light, I mean, rather, those things that flowed from the light. He gives me to understand the strange new form which He Himself has refashioned for me.... He separated me from the corrupt world and the things of this world. He put on me a robe that is immaterial and radiant, and similar sandals. After having rendered me thus, the Creator led me into a tent, a sensible one, that of my body. There He enclosed me securely. He put me back in the sensible and visible world, that I should live with those who dwell in darkness, I who had been freed from the darkness."[84]

And Nicholas Cabasilas observes:

"The future life is not entirely unknown and strange to the present life; rather, there is a certain connection between the one and the other.... And the Saints, even before death, by which they are born into the other world, have many revelations about the future life."[85]

In the *Evergetinos,* a question is asked about an event that occurs to some, whereby they are taken from the body, which for a length of time remains dead, and afterwards returns to life. (As we saw at the beginning of this work, today certain doctors have seriously occupied themselves with phenomena related to this.) To this question, St. Gregory the Dialogist (540–604) gives the following reply:

"This event, if one understands it well, . . . is a divine admonishment for man; for providentially the event is effected by the compassion of God and presented as the greatest gift of mercy, such that many, after the departure of their soul from the body, should return again to their deadened bodies: that having seen for themselves, with the eyes of their soul, the torments of Hell (which, hearing from others, they did not believe), they might thereby learn to fear [Hell].

"There once lived a monk named Peter. This monk was a disciple of a hermit Elder, Ebbasa, who led an ascetic life in a deserted and forested area. Elder Ebbasa related to his disciple Peter that before he was settled in that deserted place, he had become ill and died. However, after a short time his soul returned to its body. When he had come to himself, he assured those around him that he had seen with his eyes the torments of Hell and the countless flaming places, and that he had even seen a fair number of the rulers of this world suspended in that fire. And as he himself was being led away to be cast into that place of torment and flame, a radiant Angel suddenly appeared and prevented them from casting him into that fire. And the Angel said to him: 'Go, and mind yourself; from now on you should live with great heed.'

"After hearing this voice, the cold limbs of his body began to warm up again, and when he had completely awakened from the sleep of eternal death, he related to those present all that had happened to him.

"Afterwards he gave himself up to the most austere fasting and vigils, always recalling and fearing the torments he had seen in Hell. . . ."[86]

Another important vision of this kind was recorded by St. Metrophanes, the disciple of St. Dionysios the Orator (both of whom lived as monastics on the Holy Mountain during the sixteenth and the beginning of the seventeenth centuries). It is a vision that was seen in 1580 by a pious Christian named Demetrios, who was an inhabitant of Stratoniki, a small town in Chacidice [the Macedonian peninsula terminating in three narrow arms, one of which is Athos]. This Demetrios, after a terrible illness of fifteen days, was reduced to an apparent state of death. For hours he was thought to be dead by his relatives and neighbors; they had even wrapped him in a shroud to bury him the next morning. But suddenly he sighed and sat up on his bed. He remained in this position, without speaking or eating, for three days. Then he began to speak and relate all that which he, having been led by an Angel, had been deemed worthy to see in Paradise and Hell.[87]

So much, then, for the Middle State, the state of the soul after death and before the General Resurrection.

The Resurrection of the dead, that is, of the bodies of those who have fallen asleep—from the first to the last, of both the righteous and the sinners—, will take place at the time of the Second Coming of the God-Man Christ. The God-inspired John the Damascene says with regard to this:

"We also believe in the resurrection of the dead. For in truth it will happen, there will be a resurrection of the dead. But when we say resurrection, we mean a resurrection of bodies. For resurrection is a second standing of that which has fallen. And souls are immortal; hence, how can they rise again? For if death is defined as a separation of the soul from the body, resurrection surely is the rejoining of soul and body and the second standing of the dissolved and fallen creature. It is, then, the very body that is corrupted and dissolved that will resurrect incorruptible.

"For He who formed it in the beginning from the dust of the earth is not incapable of raising it up again after it has again been dissolved and returned to the earth from which, by the decision of the Creator, it was taken. . . .

"Therefore, there will be, indeed, *there will be* a resurrection. For God is just, and He is the rewarder of those who await Him patiently. Now, if the soul had engaged in the contests for virtue alone, then it would also be crowned alone. And if it alone indulged in pleasures, then it alone would be justly punished. But since the soul pursued neither vice nor virtue without the body, it will be just for them both together to receive that which is their due. Moreover, the divine Scriptures also witness that there will be a resurrection of bodies. . . .

"Therefore, we shall rise again, with our souls once more united to our bodies, which will have become incorrupt and put off corruption. And we shall stand before the fearful judgement seat of Christ."[88]

The resurrected bodies will be spiritual, incorruptible, and not dependent on the circumstances of this world. They will be free from bodily needs—the need for food, sleep, etc.—as well as from death and every corruption. But while the bodies of the righteous will be pure and radiant and full of divine glory (according to the Savior's words: "then shall the righteous shine forth as the sun in the kingdom of their Father"[89]), the bodies of the sinners will be impure and dark, being deprived of that divine glory, the uncreated and eternal light of God.

Comparing this resurrected body to the body that the soul comes out of at death, the Apostle Paul says:

"It is sown a natural body, and it is raised a spiritual body. There is a natural body, and there is a spiritual body. . . . Howbeit that was not first which is spiritual, but that which is natural; and afterward that which is spiritual. . . . Now this I say, brethren, that flesh and blood cannot inherit the kingdom of God; neither doth corruption inherit incorruption. Behold, I show you a mystery, . . . we shall all be changed, in a moment, in the twinkling of an eye, at the last trump: for the trumpet shall sound, and the dead shall be raised incorruptible. . . . For this corruptible must put on incorruption, and this mortal must put on immortality."[90]

In one of his homilies, St. Symeon the New Theologian says the following about the character the body will have when resurrected:

"It is raised a body, wholly spiritual and unchanging, the kind that the body of our Master Christ was after the Resurrection, Who became ... our first-born from the dead. That body was very much different from the body of Adam, the first man who was created."

Therefore, he observes, the "earth" that Christ says the righteous will then inherit will not be sensible, but spiritual. For "in what way could those who have become spiritual inherit a sensible earth? Rather, they will deserve to inherit an entirely spiritual and immaterial earth, in order to have a dwelling worthy of their special glory —they who have obtained their bodies incorporeal and have risen above everything sensory."[91] In one of his divine hymns, St. Symeon says the following about spiritual bodies:

> In the future resurrection of the dead,
> Each soul will find, according to its worth,
> A covering full of light or darkness.
> On the other hand, those souls that are pure
>   and partake of light
> Will all be in light unwaning
> But those that are impure, and the eyes of whose
>   heart
> Are blind and full of darkness,
> How will they see the divine radiance?
> . . . Consequently a darkness without light awaits
>   them.

Continuing, he says of the bodies of the righteous at the Resurrection:

> They are raised up again, glorified,
> Radiant and resplendent, as divine light.
> Being inhabited by the souls of the Saints,
> They will shine then more than the sun.

But about the bodies of sinners he writes:

> But the bodies of sinners are raised up again
> Just as they were sown in the earth:
> Muddy, stinking, full of corruption
> Thoroughly darkened, as having done the works
> Of darkness, and served as instruments of the
>   wicked sower

For every sort of evil.
These also are raised up immortal
And spiritual, but resembling the darkness.

When the bodies are resurrected, as spiritual bodies, then the General and Last Judgement will take place. After the conclusion of the Judgement, the blessedness and glory of the righteous will be fuller, while the torment of sinners will be complete: for both the righteous and the sinners will now be united with their bodies, which will also participate in the blessedness or torment.

With regard to this judgement, Jesus says:

"When the Son of man shall come in his glory, and all the holy angels with him, then shall he sit upon the throne of his glory: and before him shall be gathered all nations: and he shall separate them one from another, as a shepherd divideth his sheep from the goats: and he shall set the sheep on his right hand, but the goats on the left. Then shall the King say unto them on his right hand: Come, ye blessed of my Father, inherit the kingdom prepared for you from the foundation of the world. . . . Then shall he say also unto them on the left hand: Depart from me, ye cursed, into everlasting fire, prepared for the devil and his angels. . . . And these shall go away into everlasting punishment: but the righteous into life eternal."[93]

The various degrees of Paradise and Hell that we discussed earlier in relation to the Middle State will also exist in the unending life that will begin with the verdict of the General Judgement.[94] As in the Middle State, so also will the righteous know one another in the unending state that will follow the General Judgement. In relation to this theme, Symeon the New Theologian says:

"The Saints are all bound to see and know one another. Even those who have never seen one another physically in this world will come to be known there.

... As it is impossible for the Father never to have known the Son, or the Son the Father, so also for the Saints, who, having God dwelling within them, became gods by grace, it is in no wise possible for one not to know the other; rather, they will eternally behold each other's glory—and their own glory—, ... with unutterable exultation and joy. And this was actually demonstrated both in the old epoch, by the Prophets, and in the new one, by many of the Saints, when they called by name those whom they had never seen, and recognized those whom they had never known."[95]

One subject remains for us to touch upon: that of development or progress in the future life. Some believe that the departed's condition is unchangeable.[96] However, we have already observed that after the soul's exit from the body, in the Middle State, it may experience a certain improvement in its condition, owing to the entreaties of the Church and the prayers, acts of charity, and other good works done by relations on its behalf, and that, during this interval, the soul's deliverance from Hell is not impossible. We have also noted that, after the General Judgment, the blessedness of the righteous becomes more complete than what it was during the Middle State. The question now is whether, during the unending life after the General Judgment, there will be any advancement. With regard to those in Hell, the Church teaches that there will be no progress at all. She rejects the belief in the restoration of those in Hell as a heresy. However, as regards those in Paradise, through the mouths of the great Fathers She teaches that there will be continuous progress. When it is said that the blessedness of the righteous will be "complete" immediately after the Great Judgment, this simply means that it will be fuller than their blessedness in the Middle State.

St. John Klimakos, having in mind the righteous who have attained to spiritual love (the highest of virtues), says:

"We shall never cease to advance in love, either in the present or in the future life, continually adding light to light. And however strange what I shall say will seem to many, nevertheless it shall be said. According to the testimonies we have given, I would say that even the spiritual beings (i.e., the angels) do not lack in progress; on the contrary, they will ever receive more and more glory, more and more knowledge."[97]

This passage is in agreement with the saying of Christ: "For whosoever hath, to him shall be given, and he shall have more abundance."[98]

St. Symeon the New Theologian expresses himself in a similar manner:

"Through a clear revelation from above," he observes, "the Saints know in fact that their perfection will be endless, their progress in glory will be eternal, that in them there will be a continual increase in divine radiance, and that an end to their progress will never occur."[99]

The same thing is expressed by another great mystic of the Church, St. Gregory of Sinai, who writes:

"It is said that in the future life the Angels and the Saints will never cease to progress in the increase of divine gifts."[100]

NOTES

1. *Coevolution Quarterly* (Sausalito, Calif.), No. 14 (1977), pp. 100-107.
2. Both were published in New York.
3. Father Seraphim was a monk at the Brotherhood and Monastery of St. Herman of Alaska (in Platina, California), which he helped to found. He reposed on September 2, 1982. [His body, which lay in state, unembalmed, in temperatures near 100 degrees F., showed no sign of decay during the few days before his burial, a traditional sign of sanctity in the Orthodox Church. – *Translator's note.*] He is the author of other worthwhile theological works.
4. For example, Raymond Moody, in his book, *Life After Life*, notes that many of the instances of clinical death which he studied lasted as long as twenty minutes (pp. 29, 146-147).
5. For example, Elisabeth Kübler-Ross, in her forementioned lecture, cites an incident of three and one half hours (p. 103).
6. Raymond Moody, *Life after Life*, p. 147. Cf. Elisabeth Kübler-Ross, *supra*, p. 103.
7. *Ibid.*, p. 145.
8. Romans 5: 20-21. Cf. Acts 2: 17-18.
9. St. Matthew 6: 25. Cf. St. Luke 11: 39-40: "And the Lord said unto him, Now do ye Pharisees make clean the outside of the cup and the platter; but your inward part is full of ravening and wickedness. Ye fools, did not he that made that which is without make that which is within also?" Cf. also Romans 7:22: "For I delight in the law of God after the inward man."
10. II Corinthians 4:16.
11. Gregory Nysseni, *Opera Ascetica*, ed. Wernerus Jaeger, Johannes Cavarnos, Virginia Callahan, VIII, p. 1, Leiden, 1952.
12. [St.] Symeon the New Theologian, *Extant Works.* In the modern Greek version by Dionysios Zagoraios, second edition, Syros, 1886, p. 549.
13. St. Matthew 16:26.
14. "On the Origin of Man," 7, 9-16.
15. *Christian Morality*, 4th edition, Volos, 1957, p. 81. Cf. St. James 2:26: "For as the body without the spirit is dead, so faith without works is dead also."
16. *Handbook of Counsel*, 2nd edition, Athens, 1885, p. 33.
17. *Philokalia*, II, Athens, 1958, p. 224.
18. *Supra*, p. 42.
19. St. Ephraim the Syrian, "The Ascetic Works." In the modern Greek version by Mark D. Sakkorrafos, Athens, 1964, p. 250.

20. St. Isaac the Syrian, *The Ascetic Works*, Athens, 1961, p. 277.

21. Wisdom of Solomon 7:6; St. Luke 9:31; II Peter 1:15.

22. II Timothy 4:6; Philippians 1:23.

23. St. Ephraim the Syrian, *op. cit.*, p. 155.

24. [St.] Symeon, Archbishop of Thessalonica, *Collected Works*, Thessalonica, ca. 1960, p. 346.

25. In the *Great Octoechos.*

26. *Supra*, p. 155. Cf. p. 9: "At that time all things seek to come into your mind."

27. *Ibid.*, p. 9.

28. *Ibid.* Cf. St. Theognostos, *Philokalia*, II, p. 267 (LXI).

29. Constantine Cavarnos and Mary Barbara Zeldin, *St. Seraphim of Sarov.* In *Modern Orthodox Saints,* V, Belmont (Mass.), 1980, p. 47.

30. Hebrews 9:27.

31. St. John 5:24.

32. *Philokalia*, I, Athens, 1957, p. 273. Compare with the following passage about the Saints from St. Makarios of Egypt: "Angels stay around them and holy spirits encircle them and protect them; and when they leave the body, the choirs of Angels take up their souls to their own abode, ...and they are presented before the Lord" (*Spiritual Homilies*, Volos, 1954, p. 131).

33. *The Ladder*, Constantinople, 1883, "Step Nine (L)" p. 67.

34. *Ibid.* Cf. the following from St. Athanasios' life of St. Anthony the Great: "For once, when [St. Anthony was] about to eat, having risen up to pray about the ninth hour, he perceived that he was caught up in the spirit, and, wonderful to tell, he stood and saw himself, as it were, from outside himself, and that he was led in the air by certain ones. Next, certain bitter and terrible beings stood in the air and wished to hinder him from passing through. But when his conductors opposed them, they demanded whether he was not accountable to them. And when they wished to sum up the account from his birth, Anthony's conductors stopped them, saying, 'The Lord hath wiped out the sins from his birth, but from the time that he became a monk, and devoted himself to God, it is permitted for you to make a reckoning.' Then when they accused him and could not convict him, his way was free and unhindered. And immediately he saw himself, as it were, coming and standing by himself, and again he was Anthony as before" (Saint Athanasios the Great, "Life of St. Anthony." *Library of the Greek Fathers and Ecclesiastical Authors*, XXXIII, Athens, 1963, p. 43).

35. St. John 5:22. Cf. Acts 10:42: "It is he [Jesus Christ] which was ordained of God to be the Judge of quick and dead." See also St. Clement of Rome, "Second Epistle to the Corinthians": "Brethren, we must think of Jesus Christ, as of God, as of 'the Judge of the living and the dead' " (I, i).

36. *The Twenty-Nine Discourses of our Holy Father Isaiah*, Volos, 1962, p. 37.

37. *Ibid.*, pp. 99-100.

38. *Philokalia*, I, p. 272.

39. From Friday Vespers, Tone 2.

40. January 27, commemoration of the disinterment of the Relics of our Father among the Saints, John Chrysostomos, Ode 5 of the Matins service.

41. *Supra*, pp. 99-100. Cf. St. John Klimakos: "Make the holy powers [Angels] your friends, who can help you at the hour of your death, if they become your friends" (*The Ladder*, "Step Three (XVI),"p.25.

42. *Supra*, p. 255.

43. *Supra*, pp. 99-100.

44. [St.] Symeon of Thessalonica, *op. cit.*, p. 346. Christ refers to this seizing of the soul by the demons in His parable of the greedy rich man, when he says: "Thou fool, this night thy soul shall be required of thee" (St. Luke 12:20).

45. See St. Luke 16:22.

46. St. Symeon of Thessalonica, *op cit.*, pp. 345-346.

47. *Library of the Greek Fathers and Ecclesiastical Authors*, XXXIII, Athens, 1963, pp. 41-42.

48. See Photios Kontoglou, *An Exposition of the Orthodox Faith*, I, Athens, 1966, p. 386.

49. *Supra*, p. 56.

50. "An Exact Exposition of the Orthodox Faith" (II, 18). See also II, 17 & 29, as well as the following words of St. Makarios of Egypt: "Each of these, after its kind, is a body, be it Angel, or soul, or demon. Subtile though they are, still in substance, character, and image..., they are subtile bodies, even as this body of ours is in substance a heavy body" (*Spiritual Homilies*, p. 36).

51. *Supra*, p. 346.

52. *Ibid.*

53. *Evergetinos*, I, Athens, 1981, p. 138.

54. *Ibid.*, p. 85.

55. This is probably by the blessed Archbishop Theophilos the Confessor, Archbishop of Ephesus, who was an opponent of iconoclasm.

56. *Evergetinos*, I, p. 161.

57. *Study Concerning the Immortality of the Soul and the Ho-*

ly Memorial Services, Athens, 1901, pp. 170, 173.
58.   *Supra,* p. 349.
59.   *Our Holy Father Dorotheos: Words on Contrition,* Volos, 1960, p. 89.
60.   St. Luke 16: 23-25.
61.   *Ibid.,* 27-28.
62.   *Dogmatic Theology of the Orthodox Eastern Church,* 2nd edition, Athens, 1956, p. 411.
63.   *Library of the Greek Fathers and Ecclesiastical Authors,* XXXIII, p. 195.
64.   St. Makarios of Egypt, *Spiritual Homilies,* p. 233.
65.   *Ibid.,* "Homily XL." pp. 190-191. Cf. St. Matthew 18:4: "Whosoever therefore shall humble himself as this little child, the same is greatest in the kingdom of heaven." See also, St. Luke 12: 47-48: "And that servant, which knew his lord's will, and prepared not himself, neither did according to his will, shall be beaten with many stripes. But he that knew not, and did commit things worthy of stripes, shall be beaten with few stripes."
66.   *Philokalia,* IV, Athens, 1961, pp. 36-38.
67.   *Supra,* p. 279. Cf. St. Symeon of Thessalonica: "We are obliged to believe that the souls of sinners and unbelievers are in Hades, in places of darkness and tribulations, ...and, according to the degree of their sins and of their unbelief, they are ruled over by the demons and, being tormented, afflicted by them" (*Collected Works,* pp. 346-347.)
68.   14: 2-3.
69.   16:28.
70.   *Supra,* p. 89.
71.   "Bodily place," St. John Damascene observes, "is the limit of that which contains, by which that which is contained is contained: for example, the air contains but the body is contained. But it is not the whole of the containing air which is the place of the contained body, but the limit of the containing air, where it comes into contact with the contained body.... But there is also mental place where mind is active, and mental and incorporeal nature exists: where mind dwells and energizes and is contained not in a bodily but in a mental fashion.... But the angel [and the soul] is circumscribed alike in time (for His being had commencement) and in place (but mental space, as we said above) and in apprehension ("An Exact Exposition of the Orthodox Faith," I, 14 [See Eerdmans, *Nicene and Post Nicene Fathers,* 2nd series, IX, pp. 15-16, for the English text; the Greek text is correspondingly complex —*Trans.*]). As regards time in the spiritual world, I should note that this God-bearing Father, speaking of the resurrection of the dead, says that after the resurrection, time will be

measured, not with the units of days and nights, but that it, "rather, shall be a day without evening of the sun of righteousness, for the righteous a day brilliantly shining, but for the sinners a deep and unending night" (*Ibid.* [Greek text], II, 16).

72. "Concerning the Departed Faithful: That the Liturgies and Charities Performed for Them are to Their Benefit," in St. John Damascene, "On the Orthodox Faith," p. 226.

73. *The Treasury of Damaskinos the Studite*, Nik. K. Papadopoulos, Athens, 9th edition, "Discourse XV," p. 224.

74. *Study Concerning the Immortality of the Soul and Holy Memorial Services, op. cit.,* p. 173. See also Haralampos D. Basilopoulos, *The Benefits of Memorial Services [for the Dead]*, Athens, 1976.

75. *Ibid.,* p. 84.

76. *Ibid.,* p. 85.

77. *Ibid.*

78. *Ibid.,* p. 74.

79. *Ibid.,* p. 83.

80. *Ibid.*

81. *Ibid.,* p. 196. See St. Symeon of Thessalonica: "And if, then, some have sinned moderately, it suffices for them only to depart this life in repentance, then through the means of the most sacred Sacrifice, good works, works of mercy, and other such, they may come to be free even before the advent of the Judge" (*Collected Works*, p. 347).

82. 12: 2-4.

83. *Supra*, p. 69.

84. St. Symeon, *Extant Works*, II, p. 3.

85. *The Christian Life*, Athens, 1954, pp. 10-11.

86. *Evergetinos*, I, p. 123.

87. A description of this vision was published in *Tradition*, I, 6 (1977), 368-370, II, 7 (1978), 38-41.

88. "An Exact Exposition of the Orthodox Faith" (IV, 104).

89. St. Matthew 13: 43.

90. I Corinthians 15: 44, 46, 50-54.

91. *Extant Works*, pp. 213-214.

92. *Supra*, II, p. 72.

93. St. Matthew 25: 31-34, 41, 46.

94. See St. Symeon the New Theologian, *Extant Works*, II, p. 72.

95. *Ibid.*, I, pp. 230, 232.

96. See, for example, Androutsos, *op. cit.*, p. 409.

97. *The Ladder*, "Step Twenty-Six," pp. 141-142.

98. St. Matthew 13:12.

99. *Extant Works*, II, p. 41.

100. *Philokalia*, IV, p. 38. Who is it that says this, in the passage cited? Undoubtedly, St. Gregory of Sinai is referring to the Fathers of the Church. He makes no objection, so he therefore shares this view.

II

JESUS CHRIST ON THE SOUL

The Gospel According to St. Matthew

10:28:

And fear not them which kill the body, but are not able to kill the soul: but rather fear him which is able to destroy both soul and body in hell.

***

16:26 :

For what is a man profited, if he shall gain the whole world, and lose his own soul? or what shall a man give in exchange for his soul?

***

6:25, 33 :

Take no thought for your life, what ye shall eat, or what ye shall drink; nor yet for your body, what ye shall put on. Is not the life [soul] more than meat, and the body than raiment?... But seek ye first the kingdom of God, and his righteousness; and all these things shall be added unto you.

The Gospel According to St. Luke

9:56:

For the Son of man is not come to destroy men's lives [souls], but to save them.

***

12: 16-20:

And he [Jesus] spake a parable unto them, saying, The ground of a certain rich man brought forth plentifully: And he thought within himself, saying, What shall I do, because I have no room where to bestow my fruits? And he said, This will I do: I will pull down my barns, and build greater; and there will I bestow all my fruits and my goods. And I will say to my soul, Soul, thou hast much goods laid up for many years; take thine ease, eat, drink, and be merry. But God said unto him, Thou fool, this night thy soul shall be required of thee.

***

21:19:

In your patience possess ye your souls.

St. John 15: 12-13, St. Luke 9:24:

This is my commandment, That ye love one another, as I have loved you. Greater love hath no man than this, that a man lay down his life for his friends.... But whosoever will lose his life for my sake, the same shall save it.

Note: In this section and in subsequent citations from the New Testament, we have used the King James version of the text to render the original Greek text cited by the author. It is both our opinion and that of Professor Cavarnos that, with a few exceptions (some of which we have noted in brackets), the King James translation best fits the meaning, tone, and style of the original Greek. Many modern Biblical scholars, often with a knowledge of Greek that does not extend to its Byzantine and present forms, and therefore working with a largely artificial understanding of the language, would not agree with this assessment. A good grasp of Greek as a living language, however, leads one inevitably to the view which we have advocated. *—Trans.*

III

THE SOUL ACCORDING TO THE FATHERS
OF THE CHURCH

St. Basil the Great

I recognize two men, one which is visible and one which is hidden within the same —invisible, the inner man. We have therefore an inner man, and we are of dual make-up. Indeed, it is truthful to say that we exist inwardly. The self is the inner man. The outer parts are not the self, but belongings of it. For the self is not the hand, but rather the rational faculty of the soul, while the hand is a part of man. Thus while the body is an instrument of man, an instrument of the soul, man, strictly speaking, is chiefly the soul. ("On the Origin of Man," VII, IX-XVI. *Sources Chrétiennes*, No. 160, by A. Smets & M. Van Esbroeck, Paris, 1970, p. 182.)

St. Gregory the Theologian

What God is in relation to the soul, so is the soul in realtion to the body, when the soul herself has instructed the servile matter, and acquainted her co-servant with God. ("In Defense of His Flight to Pontus,"Migne, *P.G.*, XXXV, 428.)

***

The soul is from God and divine, and partakes of the benefits from on high. (*Ibid.,* p. 424.)

St. Makarios of Egypt

The soul is a spiritual creation, great and beautiful, marvelous and good, a likeness and image of God. (*Spiritual Homilies*, "Homily I," Volos, 1954, p. 23.)

***

The Christian knows that the soul is greater in worth than all other created things. (*Ibid.*, "Homily VI," p. 101.)

***

So great then is the soul, and how it has been honored by God! Indeed, God and the Angels seek it for their own communion and kingdom; Satan and his powers, however, seek it for their own place. (*Ibid.*, p. 102.)

***

The soul has a form similar to that of the Angel. For, as the Angels have form, and the outer man has form, so also the inner man has a form resembling that of the Angels and the outer man. (*Ibid.*, "Homily VIII," p.56.)

***

Just as these bodily eyes see the sun, so those who are enlightened see the form of the soul, though indeed few Christians see this. (*Ibid.*)

***

For it is beneficial for all to know this, that there are eyes more inward than these [physical] eyes and a hearing more inward than this [physical] hearing. And as these [physical] eyes sensibly see and recognize the face of a friend or loved one, so, too, those of worthy and faithful soul, enlightened spiritually by divine light, see and know the *true* friend and sweetest and much-desired bridegroom, the Lord. (*Ibid*, "Homily XXIX," pp. 161-162.)

St. John Damascene

Every man is a combination of soul and body.... The soul is a living substance, simple and without body, invisible to the bodily eyes by virtue of its peculiar nature, immortal, rational, spiritual, without form [i.e., without a visible shape, such as that of the body], using the bodily organ, in which it occasions growth, sensibility, and productiveness. The mind is not something separate from the soul, but is its purest part, since what the eyes are to the body, such is the mind to the soul. The soul is independent, with a will and energy of its own, and changeable, that is, capable of altering itself, since it is a created thing [and thus has free will]. ("An Exact Exposition of the Orthodox Faith," III, 3, II, 29.)

***

The good Angel is a spirit; and the demon is a spirit; so, too, is the soul a spirit. (*Ibid.,* I, 14.)

St. Symeon the New Theologian

As much as the soul is more honored than the body, so much so the rational man rises above the entirety of the visible world. Seeing the magnitude of all created things within the world, do not think, O man, that they are therefore higher in honor than you; but beholding the grace which has been given to you and understanding the value of your rational soul, glorify God, Who has honored you above all visible things. (*Philokalia*, III, Athens, 1960, pp. 255-256.)

St. Gregory Palamas

Not only in this has man been created more in the image of God than the Angels, that he has a cohesive and enlivening power within him (restraining and enlivening his body), but also by virtue of his ability to rule. For within the nature of our souls, there is, on the one hand, that which commands and exercises sovereignty, and, on the other hand, that part which by nature serves and obeys: there are will, desire, sensibility, and all the other powers of the soul which, together with the mind, were created by God.... [Yet] since we have within us that which commands, God has granted us lordship over all the earth. (*Philokalia*, IV, Athens, 1961, p. 156.)

Note. The translations in the foregoing section are, for the most part, direct translations from the Greek. We have used some standard English references in some instances for parts of the quotes, to make them more familiar to the reader, when this did not compromise the meaning of the original Greek. The textual references at the end of each passage, however, refer to the Greek original of each passage. *—Trans.*

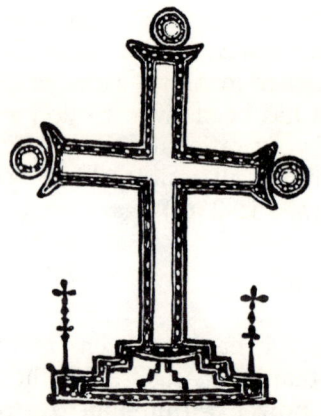

IV

THE SURVIVAL OF THE SOUL AFTER DEATH ACCORDING TO HOLY SCRIPTURE

I Kings 28: 3-19:

And Samuel died, and all Israel lamented for him, and they bury him in his city, in Armathaim. And Saul had removed those who had in them divining spirits, and the wizards, out of the land. And the Philistines assemble themselves, and come and encamp in Sonam: and Saul gathers all the men of Israel, and they encamp in Gelbue. And Saul saw the camp of the Philistines, and he was alarmed and his heart was greatly dismayed. And Saul enquired of the Lord: and the Lord answered him not by dreams, nor by manifestations, nor by prophets.

Then Saul said to his servants, Seek for me a woman who has in her a divining spirit, and I will go to her, and enquire of her: and his servants said to him, Behold there is a woman who has in her a divining spirit at Aendor.

And Saul disguised himself, and put on other raiment, and he goes, and two men with him, and they come to the woman by night: and he said to her, Divine to me, I pray thee, by the divining spirit within thee, and bring up to me him whom I shall name to thee. And the woman said to him, Behold now, thou knowest what Saul has done, how he has cut off those who had in them divining spirits, and the wizards from the land, and why dost thou spread a snare for my life to destroy it? And Saul swore to her and said, As the Lord lives, no injury shall come upon thee on this account. And the woman said, Whom shall I bring up to thee? and he said, Bring up to me Samuel.

And the woman saw Samuel, and cried out with a loud voice: and the woman said to Saul, Why hast thou deceived me? for thou art Saul. And the king said to her, Fear not; tell me whom thou hast seen. And the woman said to him, I saw gods ascending out of the earth. And he said to her, What didst thou perceive? and she said to him, An upright man ascending out of the earth, and he was clothed with a mantle. And Saul knew that this was Samuel, and he stooped with his face to the earth, and did obeisance to him.

And Samuel said, Why hast thou troubled me, that I should come up? And Saul said, I am greatly distressed, and the Philistines war against me, and God has departed from me, and no longer hearkens to me either by the hand of prophets or by dreams: and now I have called thee to tell me what I should do. And Samuel said, Why askest thou me, whereas the Lord has departed from thee, and taken part with thy neighbor? And the Lord has done to thee, as the Lord spoke by me; and the Lord will rend thy kingdom out of thy hand, and will give it to thy neighbor David, because thou didst not hearken to the voice of the Lord, and didst not execute his fierce anger upon Amalec, therefore the Lord has done this thing to thee today. And the Lord shall deliver Israel with thee into the hands of the Philistines, and tomorrow thou and thy sons with thee shall fall, and the Lord shall deliver the army of Israel into the hands of the Philistines.

III Kings 17: 17-24:

And it came to pass afterward, that the son of the woman the mistress of the house was sick; and his sickness was very severe, until there was no breath left in him. And she said to Eliu, What have I to do with thee, O man of God, hast thou come in to me to bring my sins to remembrance, and to slay my son?

And Eliu said to the woman, Give me thy son. And he took him out of her bosom, and took him up to the chamber in which he himself lodged, and laid him on the bed. And Eliu cried aloud, and said, Alas, O

Lord, the witness of the widow with whom I sojourn, hast thou brought evil for her in slaying her son. And he breathed on the child thrice, and called on the Lord, and said, O Lord my God, let, I pray thee, the soul of this child return to him. And it was so, and the child cried out, and he brought him down from the upper chamber into the house, and gave him to his mother; and Eliu said, See, thy son lives. And the woman said to Eliu, Behold, I know that thou art a man of God, and the word of the Lord in thy mouth is true.

Osee 13:14:

I will deliver them out of the power of Hades, and will redeem them from death: where is thy penalty, O death? O Hades, where is thy sting?

Ecclesiastes 12: 5-7:

Because man has gone to his eternal home, and the mourners have gone about the market: before the silver cord be let go, or the choice gold be broken, or the pitcher be broken at the fountain, or the wheel run down to the cistern; before the dust also return to the earth as it was, and the spirit return to God who gave it.

Wisdom 3: 1-10:

But the souls of the righteous are in the hand of God, and there shall be no torment touch them. In the sight of the unwise they seemed to die: and their departure is taken for misery, and their going from us to be utter destruction: but they are in peace. For though they be punished in the sight of men, yet is their hope full of immortality.

And having been a little chastised, they shall be greatly rewarded: for God proved them, and found them worthy of himself. As gold in the furnace hath he tried them and received them as a burnt offering.

And in the time of their visitation they shall shine, and run to and fro like sparks among the stubble. They shall judge the nations, and have dominion over the people, and their Lord shall reign forever. They that put their trust in him shall understand the truth: and such as be faithful in love shall abide with him: for grace and mercy is to his saints, and he hath care for his elect. But the ungodly shall be punished according to their own imaginations, which have neglected the righteous, and forsaken the Lord.

Wisdom of the Son of Sirach 38:23:

Be comforted for the dead when his spirit is departed from him.

The Gospel According to St. Luke

20:38:

For he is not a God of the dead, but of the living: for all live unto him.

***

8: 49-50, 54-55:

There cometh one from the ruler of the synagogue's house, saying to him, Thy daughter is dead.... But when Jesus heard it, he answered him, saying, Fear not: believe only and she shall be made whole. And when he went into the house..., he...took her by the hand, and called, saying, Maid, arise. And her spirit came again, and she arose straightway: and he commanded to give her meat [food].

***

16: 22-23:

And it came to pass, that the beggar died, and was carried by the angels into Abraham's bosom: the rich man also died and was buried: and in hell he lift up his eyes, being in torments, and seeth Abraham afar off, and Lazarus in his bosom.

***

23:42-44:

And he said unto Jesus, Lord, remember me when thou comest into thy kingdom. And Jesus said unto him, Verily, I say unto thee, To day shalt thou be with me in paradise.

Acts of the Apostles 7: 55-60:

[The Protomartyr and Apostle Stephen, shortly before his falling-alseep, that is, his death,] ...being full of the Holy Spirit, looked up stedfastly into heaven and saw the glory of God, and Jesus standing on the right hand of God, and said, Behold I see the heavens opened, and the Son of man standing on the right hand of God. Then they [his persecutors] cried out with a loud voice, and stopped their ears, and ran upon him with one accord, and cast him out of the city, and stoned him: and the witnesses laid down their clothes at a young man's feet, whose name was Saul. And they stoned Stephen, calling upon God, and saying, Lord Jesus, receive my spirit. And he kneeled down, and cried with a loud voice, Lord, lay not this sin to their charge. And when he had said this, he fell asleep.

II Corinthians 5: 1-2:

For we know that if our earthly house of this tabernacle were dissolved, we have a building of God, an house not made with hands, eternal in the heavens.

Hebrews 12: 18-23:

For ye are not come unto the mount that might be touched, and that burned with fire, nor unto blackness, and darkness, and tempest, and the sound of a trumpet, and the voice of words; which voice they that heard intreated that the word should not be spoken to them anymore, ...but ye are come unto mount Sion, and unto the city of the living God, the heavenly Jerusalem, and to an innumerable company of angels, to the general assembly and church of the firstborn, which are written in heaven, and to God the Judge of all, and to the spirits of just men made perfect.

I Peter 3: 18-19:

For Christ also once suffered for sins, the just for the unjust, that he might bring us to God, being put to death in the flesh, but quickened by the Spirit: by which also he went and preached unto the spirits in prison [i.e., Hades].

Revelation

6:9-11:

And when he had opened the fifth seal, I saw under the altar the souls of them that were slain for the word of God, and for the testimony which they held: and they cried with a loud voice, saying, How long, O Lord, holy and true, dost thou not judge and avenge our blood on them that dwell on the earth? And white robes were given unto everyone of them; and it was said unto them, that they should rest yet for a little season, until their fellowservants also and their brethren, that should be killed as they were, should be fulfilled.

***

14:13:

And I heard a voice from heaven saying unto me, Write, Blessed are the dead which die in the Lord from henceforth: Yea, saith the Spirit, that they may rest from their labours; and their works do follow them.

Note: In this section and in subsequent citations from the Old Testament, Professor Cavarnos has used the *Septuagint*, the authoritative text of the Old Testament used by the Greek Orthodox Church. Therefore, some of the Old Testamental references may differ from those in other texts, including the King James version, which we have used for New Testamental references. Our English translations, with minor corrections (in brackets) where needed, are taken from the Zondervan 1978 printing of Brenton's standard parallel text, *The Septuagint Version of the Old Testament and Apocrypha: Greek and English.* —Trans.

V

THE FATHERS OF THE CHURCH ON THE
IMMORTALITY OF THE SOUL

*The unknown Father who wrote the Epistle
to Diognetus (second century A.D.)*

The soul dwells in the body, but is not of the body.... The soul, being invisible, is guarded in a visible body.... The soul has been confined within the body, but it restrains the body.... The soul dwells in a mortal tabernacle, but is immortal. ("Epistle to Diognetus," IV, *Library of the Greek Fathers and Ecclesiastical Authors*, II, pp. 253-254.)

St. Justin the Philosopher and Martyr

Souls are conscious after death. ("Apology I," *Library of the Greek Fathers and Ecclesiastical Authors*, III, p. 171.)

***

God is incorruptible [immortal] by His very nature; the soul is also incorruptible by the will of the Creator. ("Gentile Questions to Christians," *Library of the Greek Fathers and Ecclesiastical Authors*, IV, p. 181. This discourse, though it is considered a doubtful work of St. Justin, constitutes a precise statement of his pertinent teachings, as found in his recognized works.)

St. Anthony the Great

A true man is one who understands that the body is corruptible and short-lived. Such a man also understands what the soul is: divine and immortal. (*Philokalia*, I, p. 21.)

***

As regards the body, man is mortal; however, as regards the mind and reason, he is immortal. (*Ibid.*, p. 19.)

St. Makarios of Egypt

It was not of Michael and Gabriel, the Archangels, that He [God] said, "Let us make them after our image and likeness" (Gen. 1:26), but of the spiritual substance of man, I mean, his immortal soul. (*Spiritual Homilies*, "Homily XV," Volos, 1954, p. 93.)

***

If He [God] was moved to such compassion over bodies that were to be dissolved and die, and did with eager kindness for each supplicant the thing that he desired, how much more will He do for an immortal, imperishable, incorruptible soul, laboring under the disease of ignorance, wickedness, unbelief, unconcern, and all the other maladies of sin. (*Ibid.*, "Homily IV," p. 43.)

***

The immortal soul is a precious vessel! See how great the heavens and the earth are, and God was not satisfied with them, but only with thee. Consider thy dignity and nobility.... (*Ibid.*, "Homily XXVI, p. 140.)

St. Athanasios the Great

Since the soul moves itself, it follows that, after putting aside the body, it should continue to move itself. For it is not the soul that dies, but the body, which dies after the departure of the soul. ("Against the Heathen," *P.G.*, XXXIII, 25, 65B.)

***

The soul considers and thinks of things that are eternal and immortal because it is immortal. (*Ibid.*, *P.G.*, 25, 68B.)

St. Basil the Great

As for me, if anyone were to mention the longevity of Tithonus, or of the Arganthonius [a mountain range in Asia Minor —*Trans.*], or of Mathusala, who lived longer than any other man —for it is reported that he lived a thousand years, minus only thirty—, or if someone were to calculate all the time that has passed since the moment man was created, I would laugh at all of this, as at a childish idea; for I look to a long and ageless eternity, the end of which the mind is not capable of conceiving, just as the mind cannot contemplate an end to the immortal soul. ("Discourse to the Young as to the Benefit of Greek Letters," I, 4.)

St. Gregory the Theologian

For us, that which is endangered [by sin] is the salvation of the soul. For the soul is blessed and immortal, and, as an immortal thing, it will be punished or lauded for its wickedness or its virtue. ("In Defense of His Flight to Pontus," *P.G.*, XXXV, p. 437.)

St. John Chrysostom

That we have an immortal soul, and that we are accountable and shall give answer for our deeds, and that we will appear before the fearful tribunal —these things are believed by the minds [of true Christians], and they have arranged the whole of their lives in accord with these hopes, and have risen above every worldly imagination, having been instructed by the Divine Scriptures. ("Homilies on the Statues," XIX, *P.G.*, XLIX, p. 189.)

St. Mark the Ascetic

Enfeeble, O Child, your youthly flesh, and in this way enhance your immortal soul. (*Philokalia*, I, Athens, 1957, p. 133.)

St. Abba Dorotheos

At the hour that God made man, he also sowed the virtues within him, as it is said: "Let us make man in our image, after our likeness." He said "in our image" because he made the soul imperishable and self-ruling. ("Sayings," Volos, 1960, p. 91.)

St. John Klimakos

The whole world is not equal in worth to the soul, for the world passes away, while the soul is imperishable and remains imperishable. (*The Ladder*, "Step XXXI," Constantinople, 1883, p. 179.)

St. John Damascene

Every man is said to be in the image of God by virtue of the dignity of the mind and soul, that is, because the characteristics of the mind and of the entirety of the soul are indestructibility, invisibility, immortality, and self-rule. (*Philokalia*, II, Athens, 1958, p. 238.)

***

Death is a separation of the soul from the body. That body, then, that was fashioned from the dust, when it is separated from the soul, returns to the earth from which it was taken, where, corrupting, it dissolves. But the soul, being immortal, proceeds to the place that God commands, or rather, to the place that it prepared for itself when it was still in the body. For, according to the manner that a man lives, so shall he there receive. ("Barlaam and Iosaph," *Loeb Classical Library,* III, p. 63.)

St. Symeon the New Theologian

If you will occasion to examine carefully, you will plainly know that of all of the things of this world, nothing is steadfast or certain amongst all that is apparent, save the soul of man; but I should say that the soul appears only invisibly, that is, spiritually, and so is believed to be immortal. (*Extant Works*, Syros, 1886, p.

142.)

***

The soul is spiritual and by nature immortal. (*Ibid.*, p. 149.)

***

Why, having an immaterial and wholly immortal soul, do we look to matter —to this corruptible matter? (*Ibid.*, II, p. 31 [cf. p. 64].)

Neketas Stethatos

I am an image of God, both with regard to the soul, which is spiritual and immortal and rational, and in having a mind that is the father of reason and indivisible and of one essence with the soul. (*Philokalia*, III, Athens, 1960, p. 306.)

St. Gregory Palamas

Every rational and spiritual nature, whether it be angelic or human, has life, by which it remains immortal and unsusceptible to corruption. (*Philokalia*, IV, Athens, 1961, p. 143.)

St. Cosmas Aitolos

Man and woman did not exist in this world. God took dust from the earth and fashioned a man like us, and He breathed into it, granting it an immortal soul.... And we should meditate on what the body and soul are. The body is dust and tomorrow will be eaten by worms, and it is necessary that the soul rejoice forever in Paradise, should it do what is good, or burn in Hell, if it does what is bad. (Augustine Kantiotis, *St. Cosmas Aitolos*, 3rd edition, Athens, 1966, p. 105-106.)

***

The All-Good God commanded, and this world came to be, and He made a man and a woman like unto

us: the body from the dust and the soul angelic and immortal. (*Ibid.,,* p. 157.)

***

Let us think about our soul, which is greater in honor than all the world. Let us eat and drink only what is
necessary, and, likewise, let us care only that we have
sufficient clothing. And let us spend the rest of our time
on the soul, that we may make it a bride of Christ. Then
will we be properly called men and earthly angels. But if
we seek after how we might eat, drink, sin, and adorn
the body, which tomorrow will be eaten by worms, then
we should not be called men, but animals. (*Ibid.,,* p.
105.)

St. Athanasios of Paros

It is said that the soul of man was created in the
image of God. It is called such an image by virtue of
its being bodiless, immaterial, powerful, invisible, and
self-ruling. For God is all of these things, though for a
better reason. For God is truly both immortal and the
only one who is immortal by nature. Consequently, the
soul of man, as the image of God, is also immortal —not
of course by nature, but by Grace. (*Synopsis, Being a
Collection of the Divine Dogmas of the Faith*, Leipzig,
1806, p. 266.)

***

In one word, the whole of the divine Scripture, both
the Old Testament and the New, proclaims the immortality of the soul, and it would be an arduous task if I
wished to enumerate all of the references to this in
the Scriptures. (*Ibid.,* p. 268.)

***

Man is not only body, but soul also. And the soul
does not corrupt with the body, but remains immortal. ("In Reply," Athens, 1866, p. 6.)

St. Nikodemos the Hagiorite

The soul and the body, my brothers, are like two comrades that God has placed in this world, that they might be dealt with, and that each one might receive the portion of time proper to his innate worth. The soul, being immaterial, immortal, and consequently superior to the body, ought to take a larger share of our time; while the body, being material and mortal, and consequently inferior to the soul, ought to receive a smaller share. (*Christian Morality*, Volos, 1957, p. 305.)

***

Therefore, transfer the desire which you now have to adorn the outer and unreal man to the inner and true man, and adorn him with virtue. For it is great ignorance to adorn the mortal body, which exists today and tomorrow is not, and to ignore your soul, which is immortal. (*Ibid.,* p. 81.)

***

You have nothing better than this soul; you have nothing of greater worth than this immortal soul. (*Spiritual Exercises*, Volos, 1950, p. 305.)

St. Nectarios of Aegina

The immortality of the soul is truly written in the heart of man, and as soon as the spirit is activated in the mind, it discovers this, reads it, and accepts it. (*Study Concerning the Immortality of the Soul*, Athens, 1901, p. 14.)

***

Moreover, man's ardent desire for the highest good, which he will exert every care and concern to obtain, testifies to the soul's immortality.... Hoping in the enjoyment of the highest good, man believes that he has an immortal soul. Mystically, God informs man of this; the goodness of God, revealed in all, persuades him that he has an immortal soul. (*Ibid.,* p. 14, 43.)

***

According to true Orthodox belief, the human nature has two components: 1) the material and corruptible body; and 2), the immaterial, incorruptible, and immortal soul. This is proclaimed by Scripture; this is witnessed by the Fathers; this is confessed and taught by the Church. (*Ibid.,* p. 21.)

Note: The foregoing passages have, whenever possible, been taken from existing English translations. We have felt it best, given the controversy regarding life after death that has been created in some Orthodox circles, to offer standard renderings that a non-Greek-reading observer might consult. We have made changes in these translations only where absolutely required by the Greek texts. And since the English passages are drawn from so many different sources, we have thought it best to provide references only for the original Greek texts, which should also aid those who are able to read these original passages.

We might also note that, despite the absence of any such misunderstanding among scholars and thoughtful Orthodox, both in Greece and America factions have called into question the writings of St. Nectarios, accusing him of writing from a Western bias or of being inadequate in his theological knowledge. Dr. Cavarnos has no doubt included the writings of this modern Saint simply because St. Nectarios is wholly within the tradition of the great Fathers, was the director of a prestigious theological training school, and was a theological thinker of such depth that his detractors unfortunately are unable to grasp the significance of his writings. *–Trans.*

VI

THE IMMORTALITY OF THE SOUL IN ORTHODOX HYMNOGRAPHY

The Apolytikion *sung in commemoration of St. Pata-pios, St. Markellos, and other Fathers of the desert:*

In thee, O Father, was faithfully preserved the quality of being according to the Image. For thou didst take up the Cross and follow Christ. In so doing, thou didst teach us to heed not the flesh, for it passeth away, but to care for the soul as a thing immortal. Therefore, O St. Patapios, thy spirit rejoiceth with the Angels.

An Apolytikion, *similar to the foregoing, sung in memory of St. Mary of Egypt, St. Matrona, and other women monastics:*

In thee, O Mother, was faithfully preserved the quality of being according to the Image. For thou didst take up the Cross and follow Christ. In so doing, thou didst teach us to heed not the flesh, for it passeth away, but to care for the soul as a thing immortal. Therefore, O St. Mary, thy spirit rejoiceth with the angels.

Troparion *chanted at the Vespers of Sunday of the Plagal of the fourth tone, from the* Great Octoechos:

Being immortal, O my soul, be not submerged in the waves of life; arise and cry to thy Benefactor: O God, cleanse me and save me.

VII

HOLY SCRIPTURE ON THE RESURRECTION
OF THE DEAD AND THE SECOND COMING

Psalm 103: 29-30 :

Thou wilt take away their breath, and they shall fail, and return to their dust. Thou shalt send forth thy Spirit, and they shall be created; and thou shalt renew the face of the earth.

Isaiah 26:19 :

The dead shall rise, and they that are in the tombs shall be raised.

Ezekiel 27: 1-10 :

And the hand of the Lord came upon me, and the Lord brought me forth by the Spirit, and set me in the midst of the plain, and it was full of human bones. And he led me round about them every way: and, behold, there were very many on the face of the plain, very dry.

And he said to me, Son of man, will these bones live? and I said, O Lord God, thou knowest this. And he said to me, Prophesy upon these bones, and thou shalt say to them, Ye dry bones, hear the word of the Lord. Thus saith the Lord to these bones; Behold, I will bring upon you the breath of life: and I will lay sinews upon you, and will bring up flesh upon you, and will spread skin upon you, and will put my Spirit into you, and ye shall live; and ye shall know that I am the Lord.

So I prophesied as the Lord commanded me: and it came to pass that while I was prophesying, that, behold, there was a shaking, and the bones approached each one to his joint. And I looked, and, behold, sinews and flesh grew upon them, and skin came upon them above: but there was no breath in them. And he said to me, Prophesy to the wind, Thus saith the Lord; Come from the four winds, and breathe upon these dead men, and let them live. So I prophesied as he commanded me, and the breath entered into them, and they lived, and stood upon their feet, a very great congregation.

Daniel 12: 1-3:

And at that time Michael the great prince shall stand up, that stands over the children of thy people: and there shall be a time of tribulation, such tribulation as has not been from the time that there was a nation on the earth until that time: at that time thy people shall be delivered, even every one that is written in the book. And many of them that sleep in the dust of the earth shall awake, some to everlasting life, and some to reproach and everlasting shame. And the wise shall shine as the brightness of the firmament, and some of the many righteous as the stars for ever and ever.

II Maccabees 12: 44

For if he had not hoped that they that were slain should have risen again, it had been superfluous and vain to pray for the dead.

The Gospel According to St. Matthew

22: 29, 31-32:

Jesus answered and said unto them, Ye do err, not knowing the scripture, nor the power of God.... But as touching the resurrection of the dead, have ye not read that which was spoken unto you by God, saying, I am the God of Abraham, and the God of Isaac, and the God of Jacob? God is not the God of the dead, but of the living.

***

24: 27, 29-31,36-37, 42:

For as the lightning cometh out of the east, and shineth even unto the west; so shall also the coming of the Son of man be.... Immediately after the tribulation of those days shall the sun be darkened, and the moon shall not give her light, and the stars shall fall from heaven, and the powers of the heavens shall be shaken: and then shall appear the sign of the Son of man in heaven: and then shall the tribes of the earth mourn, and they shall see the Son of man coming in the clouds of heaven with power and great glory. And he shall send his angels with a great sound of a trumpet, and they shall gather together his elect from the four winds, from one end of the heaven to the other.... But of that day and hour knoweth no man, no, not the angels of heaven, but my Father only. But as the days of Noe were, so shall also the coming of the Son of man be.... Watch, therefore: for ye know not what hour your Lord doth come.

***

25: 34-46:

Then shall the King say unto them on his right hand, Come ye blessed of my Father, inherit the kingdom prepared for you from the foundation of the world: for I was an hungred, and ye gave me meat: I was thirsty, and ye gave me drink: I was a stranger and ye took me in: naked, and ye clothed me: I was sick and ye visited me: I was in prison, and ye came unto me. Then shall the righteous answer him, saying, Lord, when saw we thee an hungred, and fed thee? or thirsty, and gave thee drink? When saw we thee a stranger, and took thee in? or naked, and clothed thee? Or when saw we thee sick, or in prison, and came unto thee? And the King shall answer and say unto them, Verily I say unto you, Inasmuch as ye have done it unto one of the least of these my brethren, ye have done it unto me.
     Then shall he say also unto them on the left hand, Depart from me, ye cursed, into everlasting fire, prepared for the devil and his angels: for I was an hungred,

and ye gave me no meat: I was thirsty and ye gave me
no drink: I was a stranger, and ye took me not in:
naked, and ye clothed me not: sick, and in prison, and
ye visited me not. Then shall they also answer him, saying, Lord, when saw we thee an hungred, or athirst,
or a stranger, or naked, or sick, or in prison, and did not
minister unto thee? Then shall he answer them, saying,
Verily I say unto you, Inasmuch as ye did it not to one
of the least of these, ye did it not to me. And these shall
go away into everlasting punishment: but the righteous
into eternal life.

I Corinthians 15: 20, 22-23, 35-44, 46, 50-55, 58:

But now is Christ risen from the dead, and become
the firstfruits of them that slept.... For as in Adam all
die, even so in Christ shall all be made alive. But every
man in his own order: Christ the firstfruits; afterwards,
they that are Christ's at his coming....
But some man will say, How are the dead raised up?
and with what body do they come? Thou, fool, that
which thou sowest is not quickened, except it die; and
that which thou sowest, thou sowest not that body that
shall be, but bare grain, it may chance of wheat, or of
some other grain: but God giveth it a body as it hath
pleased him, and to every seed his own body. All flesh
is not the same flesh: but there is one kind of flesh of
men, another flesh of beasts, another of fishes, and another of birds. There are also celestial bodies, and bodies
terrestrial: but the glory of the celestial is one, and the
glory of the terrestrial is another. There is one glory of
the sun, and another glory of the moon, and another
glory of the stars: for one star differeth from another
star in glory. So also is the resurrection of the dead. It
is sown in corruption; it is raised in incorruption: it
is sown in dishonour; it is raised in glory: it is sown in
weakness; it is raised in power: it is sown a natural body; it is raised a spiritual body; There is a natural body,
and there is a spiritual body.... But that which is natural
[first] ; and afterward that which is spiritual.... Now
this I say, brethren, that flesh and blood cannot inherit

the kingdom of God; neither doth corruption inherit in-corruption. Behold, I shew you a mystery; We shall not all sleep, but we shall all be changed, in a moment, in the twinkling of an eye, at the last trump: for the trumpet shall sound, and the dead shall be raised incorruptible, and we shall be changed. For this corruptible must put on incorruption, and this mortal must put on immortality. So when this corruptible shall have put on incorruption, and this mortal shall have put on immortality, then shall be brought to pass the saying which is written, Death is swallowed up in victory. O death, where is thy sting? O grave, where is thy victory?... Therefore, my beloved brethren, be ye stedfast, unmoveable, always abounding in the work of the Lord, forasmuch as ye know that your labor is not in vain in the Lord.

Revelation 20: 11-15; 21: 1-5, 7-8:

And I saw a great white throne, and him that sat on it, from whose face the earth and the heaven fled away; and there was found no place for them. And I saw the dead, small and great, stand before God; and the books were opened: and another book was opened, which is the book of life: and the dead were judged out of those things which were written in the books, according to their works. And the sea gave up the dead which were in it; and death and hell delivered up the dead which were in them: and they were judged every man according to their works. And death and hell were cast into the lake of fire. This is the second death. And whosoever was not found written in the book of life was cast into the lake of fire.

And I saw a new heaven and a new earth: for the first heaven and the first earth were passed away; and there was no more sea. And I John saw the holy city, the new Jerusalem, coming down from God out of heaven, prepared as a bride adorned for her husband. And I heard a great voice out of heaven saying, Behold, the tabernacle of God is with men, and he will dwell with them, and they shall be his people, and God himself shall be with them, and be their God. And God shall wipe away all tears from their eyes; and there shall be no more death, neither sorrow, nor crying, neither shall there be any more pain: for the former things are passed away. And he that sat upon the throne said, Behold, I make all things new. And he said unto me, Write: for these words are true and faithful.... He that overcometh shall inherit all things; and I will be his God, and he shall be my son. But the fearful, and unbelieving, and the abominable, and murderers, and whoremongers, and sorcerers, and idolaters, and all liars, shall have their part in the lake which burneth with fire and brimstone: which is the second death.

BIBLIOGRAPHY

Holy Scripture (Old and New Testaments) [in Greek].

Saint Athanasios the Great, "Life of St. Anthony." *Library of the Greek Fathers and Ecclesiastical Authors* [in Greek], XXXIII, Athens, 1963.

Idem, "On Virginity, or On Asceticism," *ibid.*

St. Athanasios of Paros, "In Reply" [in Greek], Athens, 1866.

Idem, *Synopsis, Being A Collection of the Divine Dogmas of the Faith* [in Greek], Leipzig, 1806.

Androutsos, Chrestos, *Dogmatic Theology of the Orthodox Eastern Church* [in Greek], 2nd edition, Athens, 1956.

St. Basil the Great, "On the Origin of Man" ("Basile de Césarée sur l'Origine de l'homme"). *Sources Chrétiennes*, No. 160, by A. Smets & M. Van Esbroeck, Paris, 1970.

Idem, "Discourse to the Young as to the Benefit of Greek Letters." St. Basil, *The Letters*, Vol. IV, Loeb Classical Library, Cambridge (Mass.) and London, 1970.

Basilopoulos, Haralampos D., *The Benefits of Memorial Services [for the Dead]* [in Greek], Athens, 1976.

Monk Gerasimos Mikragiannanitis, "Unpublished Accounts of our holy Father Metrophan." In the periodical *Tradition* [in Greek], I, 6 (1977), 368-370, II, 7 (1978), 38-41.

Gregorii Nysseni [St. Gregory Nyssa], *Opera Ascetica,* ed. Wernerus Jaeger, Johannes Cavarnos, Virginia Callahan, VIII, p. 1, Leiden, 1952.

Abba Dorotheos, "Sayings." Ed. Sotirios N. Schoinas, in *Our Holy Father Dorotheos: Words on Contrition* [in Greek], Volos, 1960.

"The Epistle to Diognetus" (anonymous). *The Apostolic Fathers,* II, Loeb Classical Library, 1976.

Evergetinos [in Greek], I, Athens, 1981.

St. Ephraim the Syrian, "The Ascetic Works." In the modern Greek version by Mark. D. Sakkorrafos, Athens, 1864.

Abba Isaiah, "The Twenty-Nine Discourses." Ed. Sotirios Schoinas, in *The Twenty-Nine Discourses of our Holy Father Isaiah* [in Greek], Volos, 1962.

St. Isaac the Syrian, *The Ascetic Works* [in Greek], Athens, 1961.

St. John Damascene, "An Exact Exposition of the Orthodox Faith." In *[St.] John Damascene on the Orthodox Faith* [in Greek], Athens (St. Nikodemos Publications).

Idem, "Barlaam and Iosaph." *Loeb Classical Library,* 1937.

St. John Klimakos, *The Ladder* [in Greek], Constantinople, 1883.

Kantiotis, Augustine, *[St.] Cosmas Aitolos* [in Greek], 3rd edition, Athens, 1966.

Kontoglou, Photios, *An Exposition of the Orthodox Faith* [in Greek], I, Athens, 1966.

Idem, A Great Sign [in Greek], Athens, 1962.

Kübler-Ross E., "Death Does Not Exist." In *Coevolution Quarterly* (Sausalito, Calif.), No. 14 (1977), 100-107;

Idem, Questions and Answers on Death and Dying, New York and London, 1974.

St. Makarios of Egypt, *Spiritual Homilies,* Volos, 1954.

Menaion [in Greek].

Migne, *Patrologia Graeca.*

Moody, Raymond A., Jr., *Life after Life*, New York, 1977.

St. Nectarios Kefalas, Metropolitan of Pentapolis, *Study Concerning the Immortality of the Soul and the Holy Memorial Services* [in Greek], Athens, 1901.

St. Nikodemos the Hagiorite, *Spiritual Exercises* [in Greek], Volos, 1950.

Idem, Handbook of Counsel [in Greek], 2nd edition, Athens, 1885.

Idem, Christian Morality [in Greek], 4th edition, Volos, 1957.

Parakletike, or *The Great Octoechos* [in Greek].

Rose, Hieromonk Seraphim, *The Soul After Death,* Platina (Calif.), 1980.

[St.] Symeon, Archbishop of Thessalonica, *Collected Works* [in Greek], Thessalonica, ca. 1960.

[St.] Symeon the New Theologian, *Extant Works* [in Greek]. In the modern Greek version by Dionysios Zagoraios, second edition, Syros, 1886.

The Philokalia of the Holy Neptic Fathers [in Greek], I, Athens, 1957, II, 1958, IV, 1961.

The Great Horologion [in Greek].

Note: References are cited in order from the original Greek, not in alphabetical order according to the English alphabet.

INDEX OF NAMES

ABOUT THE AUTHOR

Professor Constantine Cavarnos, A.B. *(magna cum laude)*, A.M., Ph.D. (Harvard), is President of the Institute for Byzantine and Modern Greek Studies. Formerly associated with the University of Athens as a Fulbright Research Scholar, he has taught at Harvard University, the University of North Carolina, Wheaton College, Clark University, and at other major American colleges and universities.

Enjoying an international reputation for his scholarship in philosophy, Dr. Cavarnos is considered by many scholars to be one of the deans of contemporary Orthodox scholarship. His voluminous writings in Orthodox thought have appeared in print in this country and abroad, in Greek, English, and other languages. He makes his home both in Greece and the U.S.

We would ask readers to acknowledge the generosity of our benefactors, Mr. and Mrs. George B. Chapman, Jr., whose aid made this publication possible, and to pray for the repose of the soul of the servant of God, Arthouros Damaskinos, who contributed to the establishment of our Brotherhood.

St. Gregory Palamas Monastery

READERS' NOTES

Ἡ ἌΝΩ ἹΕΡΟΥΣΑΛΗΜ

DATE DUE

DEC 20 1992			
APR 1 6 2005			

HIGHSMITH   #LO-45220

Tl   eased to in-
fo   ooks, *Paths
ar   usion in its
19   om lectures
or   nguage, but
la   blessing and
er   nd Fili, who
fo   great spiri-
tu   chimandrite
Cl   early 1986
re